More praise for *Combat Self-Defense*

"The best, most concise explanation I have seen of the practical aspects and difficulties involved in training soldiers in the use of deadly force."
—Morgan Banks, former command psychologist,
1st Special Forces Operational Detachment—Delta

"Every commander, soldier and judge advocate going into harm's way must read this truly eye-opening and life-saving methodology for winning the close-quarters fight against an asymmetric threat."
—Jim Patterson, former command legal advisor to 1st Special
Forces Operational Detachment—Delta

"There is no second place prize in a gunfight. If you make your living protecting good people from bad things, this book will help you give your team the clear, blunt guidance it needs before the safeties come off and the front sights come into focus."
—Captain Chip Swicker, United States Navy

"A definite primer for those preparing to deploy in harm's way. Bo's work details the dynamics during and after a deadly encounter"
—Lieutenant Mike McKnight, Baltimore Police
Department's SWAT Commander

D1531023

COMBAT SELF-DEFENSE:
SAVING AMERICA'S WARRIORS FROM RISK-AVERSE COMMANDERS AND THEIR LAWYERS

COMBAT SELF-DEFENSE: SAVING AMERICA'S WARRIORS FROM RISK-AVERSE COMMANDERS AND THEIR LAWYERS

by David G. Bolgiano

Published by

Little White Wolf Books

For further information, please contact:
LWWBooks@aol.com

Book design by:
Arbor Books, Inc.
www.arborbooks.com

Printed in the United states

Combat Self-Defense: Saving America's Warriors
From Risk-Averse Commanders and Their Lawyers
David G. Bolgiano

1. Author 2. Title 3. Military/Army/National Defense

Library of Congress Control Number: 2006910620

ISBN 10: 0-9791824-0-9
ISBN 13: 978-0-9791824-0-2

Dedicated to John C. Hall and W. Hays Parks
True Warrior Lawyers

ACKNOWLEDGMENTS

I AM PROFOUNDLY GRATEFUL TO A HOST OF WARRIORS OUT THERE—our fellow sheepdogs—whose actions, thoughts and valor constantly humble me. There are many who have contributed background and ideas that must remain anonymous either because of their current unit of assignment or because of fear of retribution for speaking the truth concerning the topics in this book. Any good idea in this book was most likely the thoughts of others. As the old cowboy saying goes: "If you see a turtle on a fence post, you know it didn't get there all by itself."

Conversely, any mistake or wrong-headed thought is the responsibility of the author.

First, I wish to thank the following individuals who comprised my informal board of advisors for this project:

W. Hays Parks

John C. Hall

John H. Bolgiano

Eileen F. Bolgiano

Kathy E. Gates

Gary L. Harrell

Gary Greco

Jeff Rosen

Dave Grossman (to whom a special debt of gratitude must be extended for his gracious contribution of the Foreword to the book, as well as sage guidance concerning publication and editing options)

Allison Lenge

Trish Pullar

Robert Jarman
Morgan Banks
Paul Finfrock
Jim Patterson
Chip Swicker
John Taylor
Jim Larsen
Alisa James
Tim Quillin
Doug Cox

Special thanks to all past and current members of the ROE/RUF Tactical Training Seminar; all the terrific NCOs from the Air Mobility Warfare Center and the 175th Security Forces Squadron; the supporting members from the diverse Units we have trained; and, mentors—all who have contributed great concepts and feedback in the furtherance of training America's warriors to survive and win in combat. This group of sheepdogs includes—and I apologize if I missed someone—the following:

Al Goshi	Larry Tully
Jeff Kirkham	Steve DeLange
Geoff Wilcox	Nick Shoemaker
Mike McKnight	John Duly
Ethan Cole	Don Pedersen
Matt Little Sun	Frank Short
Mark Royka	Patty Granan
Jason "Doc" Marks	Pavel "Paul" Hubatka
Perri Rothemich	Eric Edgecomb
George "Butch" Rogers	Michael de Bethencourt
Tom DeMaio II	Tom Petrowski
Gary Glemboski	Tim Latterner
Chris Givvines	Kyle Siegel
Mark Berry	Tracey Riley
Jose Gordon	Dennis Dvorjak
Guy "Bud" Johnson	Greg Ahlers
Tony Lambraia	Bob Kenny
Steve Didier	John Nye

John Odom
John Tracy
Kevin Aandahl
Sean Fitzpatrick
Kevin O'Brien
Kevin Leavy
Tom Piddington
Steve Benden
Keith Mazzatenta
Kevin Govern
Kurt Kastner
Tony Parisi
Andy Weedon
Mark Leach
Lou Webster
Mark Maxwell
Mike Braun
Phil Calahan
Ash Naylor
Charlie Ochs
Darrell Philips
Joe Ross
Chris Gleason
Bert DiBella
Bob Rockwell
Rick Whittle
Sean Naylor
Jerry Teresinski
Tom Mowell
Anthony Sciaraffa

Jeff Spears
Carl Bailey
Tom Craddock
Jason Van Wagner
Greg Michelsen
Mark Kohart
Tom Falone
Jim Greer
Greg Morton
Robert Gruber
Jack Clark
Michele Vogel
Sean Conroy
Deborah Haller
Heather Smith
Jon Edwards
Chris Martin
Nate Kearns
Fred Mabardy
Frances Widdicombe
Jim Hicks
Mike Sawyers
Gary Khalil
Vic Hansen
Mike Smidt
Scott Holcomb
Chris Inglis
Chris Truitt [former 11th
SFG(A) trooper and police
officer, died June 2005]

A special thanks to commanders and members of the author's command and technical chain of command, who have provided unwavering support in an effort to find sound solutions to some of the problems described herein. And lastly, to my family members who have sacrificed much in support of this effort.

PREFACE

THE MEN AND WOMEN WHO WEAR THE UNIFORM OF OUR COUNTRY, whether in law enforcement or in the military, volunteer their services and risk their lives to protect us from those who would do us harm. By taking that responsibility to themselves, they willingly chose to stand in *our shoes* and do those things that we would otherwise have to do for ourselves. Decency implores, and the laws of our land require, that we stand in *their shoes* as we judge the manner in which they render this service to us. This book provides the view from those shoes. At the same time, it exposes and discusses the dangers that result from poorly crafted policies, inadequate training and equipment, and misguided leadership at many levels. The author makes no pretense of being "neutral and detached." Rather, like Winston Churchill, he has declined "to be neutral as between the fire and the fire brigade." Accordingly, he not only informs, but passionately pleads the case for those who protect us while we sleep…and that is a noble thing.

John C. Hall
Fredericksburg, Virginia
November 14, 2006

TABLE OF CONTENTS

Foreword 1

Chapter One 7
Chapter Two 11
Chapter Three 19
Chapter Four 25
Chapter Five 29
Chapter Six 41
Chapter Seven 47
Chapter Eight 57
Chapter Nine 63
Chapter Ten 71
Chapter Eleven 95
Chapter Twelve 105
Chapter Thirteen 109

Appendix 119

FOREWORD

On Lawyers, Sheep, Sheepdogs, and Wolves

THIS IS A TERRIBLY, PROFOUNDLY IMPORTANT BOOK. This book holds the key, the solution to a major problem that confronts America in our battle against terror in the post-9/11 era. To understand the contribution this book can make, and the fundamental problem that this book addresses, I think it may be of value for me to explain about the wolves and the sheepdogs; and the sheep and their lawyers...

One Vietnam veteran, an old retired colonel, once told me: "Most of the people in our society are sheep. They are kind, gentle, productive creatures who can only hurt one another by accident." This is true. Remember, the murder rate is six per 100,000 per year, and the aggravated assault rate is four per 1,000 per year. What this means is that the vast majority of Americans are not inclined to hurt one another.

Some estimates say that two million Americans are victims of violent crimes every year, a tragic, staggering number, perhaps an all-time record rate of violent crime. But there are almost 300 million Americans, which means that the odds of being a victim of violent crime is considerably less than one in a hundred on any given year. Furthermore, since many violent crimes are committed by repeat offenders, the actual number of violent citizens is considerably less than two million.

Thus there is a paradox, and we must grasp both ends of the situation: We may well be in the most violent times in history, but violence is still remarkably rare. This is because many Americans are kind, decent people who are not capable of hurting each other, except by accident or under extreme provocation. They are sheep.

I mean nothing negative by calling them sheep. To me it is like the pretty, blue robin's egg. Inside it is soft and gooey but someday it will grow into something wonderful. But the egg cannot survive without its hard blue shell. Soldiers, Marines, peace officers and other warriors are like that shell, and someday the civilization they protect may grow into something wonderful, something that doesn't need the shell. For now, though, they need warriors to protect them from the predators.

"Then there are the wolves," the old war veteran said, "and the wolves feed on the sheep without mercy." Do you believe there are wolves out there who will feed on the flock without mercy? You better believe it. There are evil men in this world and they are capable of evil deeds. The moment you forget that or pretend it is not so, you become a sheep. There is no safety in denial.

"Then there are sheepdogs," he went on, "and I'm a sheepdog. I live to protect the flock and confront the wolf."

If you have no capacity for violence then you are a healthy productive citizen: a sheep. If you have a capacity for violence and no empathy for your fellow citizens, then you have defined an aggressive sociopath—a wolf. But what if you have a capacity for violence, and a deep love for your fellow citizens? Then you are a sheepdog, a warrior, someone who is walking the hero's path. Someone who can walk into the heart of darkness, into the universal human phobia, and walk out unscathed.

The sheep generally are leery of the sheepdog. He looks a lot like the wolf. He has fangs and the capacity for violence. The difference, though, is that the sheepdog must not, cannot and will not *ever* harm the sheep. Any sheepdog who intentionally harms the lowliest little lamb *will* be punished and removed. The world cannot work any other way, at least not in a representative democracy or a republic such as ours.

The sheepdogs would no more misuse their fangs than a doctor would misuse his healing arts, but they yearn for the opportunity to use their gift to help others. These people, the ones who have the capacity for aggression and a love for others, are our sheepdogs. These are our warriors.

Still, the sheepdog disturbs the sheep. He is a constant reminder that there are wolves in the land. They would prefer that he didn't tell them where to go, or give them traffic tickets, or stand at the ready in the airport holding an M-16.

The sheep would much rather have the sheepdog cash in his fangs, spray paint himself white, and go, "Baa." The sheep (and the sheep lawyers) tend to put layers and layers of restrictive rules of engagement upon the warrior, attempting to use regulations to turn the sheepdog into a sheep. As you will see in this book, even in the heat of battle the sheep would restrain their sheepdogs and deny them that which must not and cannot be legally denied: the right of self-defense.

The sheep are leery of the sheepdog. Until the wolf shows up on *their* doorstep. When the wolf personally, immediately threatens the sheep and *their* loved ones, then the entire flock tries desperately to hide behind one lonely sheepdog. As Kipling said in his poem about "Tommy" the British soldier: While it's Tommy this, an' Tommy that, an' "Tommy, fall be'ind," But it's "Please to walk in front, sir," when there's trouble in the wind, There's trouble in the wind, my boys, there's trouble in the wind, O it's "Please to walk in front, sir," when there's trouble in the wind.

The students, the victims, at Columbine High School were big, tough high school students, and under ordinary circumstances they would not have had the time of day for a police officer. They were not bad kids; they just had nothing to say to a cop. When the school was under attack, however, and SWAT teams were clearing the rooms and hallways, the officers had to physically peel those clinging, sobbing kids off of them. *This* is how the little lambs feel about their sheepdog when the wolf is at the door. Look at what happened after September 11, 2001, when 3,000 Americans died violent, horrible deaths and the wolf was at the door. Remember how America, more than ever before, felt differently about their law enforcement officers and military personnel? Remember how many times you heard the word *hero*?

And how long did that last? Give credit where it's due. You still see plenty of yellow ribbons and flags out there. But many people said, "No one's come to kill me for over a year. Baa. No one's come to kill us for over five years! Baa! What are you guys with guns still doing out there? Go away and leave us alone." You see, they are sheep, and they sink back into denial. They only have two speeds: graze and stampede. But the warrior must remember. If the warrior doesn't remember, who will?

This is how the sheep and the sheepdog think differently. The sheep pretend the wolf will never come, but the sheepdog lives for that day. After the attacks on September 11, 2001, most of the sheep, that is, most citizens in America said, "Thank God I wasn't on one of those planes." The sheepdogs, the warriors, said, "Dear God, I wish I could have been on one of those planes. Maybe I could have made a difference." When you are truly transformed into a warrior and have truly invested yourself into warriorhood, you *want* to be there. You *want* to be able to make a difference.

In our nation the military must *never* forget that they answer to civilian leaders. But our leaders must also remember that they need our warriors, our sheepdogs, to hunt the wolves. Our warriors have the right to influence policy, and they have the undeniable right to self-defense. But when sheep establish restrictive, even (as this book outlines) illegal restraints upon our warriors, then in the end we will fail in this war.

While there is nothing morally superior about the sheepdog, the warrior, he *does* have one real advantage. Only one. *He* is able to survive and thrive in an environment that destroys 98 percent of the population.

There was research conducted a few years ago with individuals convicted of violent crimes. These cons were in prison for serious, predatory acts of violence: assaults, murders and killing law enforcement officers. The vast majority said that they specifically targeted victims by body language: slumped walk, passive behavior and lack of awareness. They chose their victims like big cats do in Africa, when they select one out of the herd that is least able to protect itself.

However, when there were cues given by potential victims that indicated they would not go easily, the cons said that they would walk away. If the cons sensed that the target was a "counter-predator," that is, a sheepdog, they would leave him alone unless there was no other choice but to engage.

The same thing is true of our warriors in distant lands.

Understand, again, that there is nothing morally superior about being a sheepdog; it is just what you choose to be. Also understand that a sheepdog can be a funny critter: He is always sniffing around out on the perimeter, checking the breeze, barking at things that go bump in the night, and yearning for a righteous battle. That is, the young sheepdogs yearn for a righteous battle. The old sheepdogs are a little older and wiser, but they move to the sound of the guns when needed right along with the young ones.

But in the end, only a predator can hunt a predator.

Q: What does the wolf call it when you send a sheep to get him?

A: Home delivery.

It bears repeating. We must never forget. Only a predator can hunt a predator, the predator dedicated to protecting the flock: the sheepdog.

Unfortunately, very few lawyers are sheepdogs. Even our military lawyers are seldom drawn from the ranks of our warriors. All too many of them learn as sheep. And, as you will see in this book, the sheep (and their lawyers) have put bizarre restrictions on our warriors in distant lands. Restrictions that have made the warriors believe that they cannot use deadly force. You will read of armed American warriors being robbed at gunpoint, because the lawyers have confused them and caused them to think and react like sheep. And when the wolf smells a sheep what does he do? He attacks!

You cannot read this book and deny that in many cases the sheep lawyers are trying to hobble the sheepdog. They are not evil, but they are terribly misguided meddlers, and they may well establish the foundation for defeat. Some of the cases outlined in this book will make you shake your head with disbelief, but they are true. The author of this book is a lawyer, but he is not a sheep. Many, many of our military lawyers are NOT sheep, but the influence of the sheep is pervasive and it can be debilitating if it is not controlled.

The author of this book represents the kind of steely logic and warrior guidance we need to win this war. He is not saying that our sheepdogs should be wolves. God forbid! But he is battling to let our sheepdogs be sheepdogs. He is battling for our warriors to have the warrior spirit that will keep them alive in hostile lands. And if we do not heed the guidance of this wise counselor, this warrior lawyer, I believe with all my heart that we may lose. Lose the war, and ultimately lose our nation and our way of life.

So listen, learn, and heed these words.

Dave Grossman
Lt. Col. USA (ret.)
www.killology.com
Author, "On Killing" and "On Combat"

CHAPTER ONE

DEATH TO MARPLOTS

Marplot. n. An officious meddler whose interference compromises the success of an undertaking.
- After *Marplot*, a character in *The Busy Body*, a play by Susannah Centlivre (1669-1723)

MORE SO THAN ANY TIME IN OUR HISTORY, American Soldiers, Sailors, Airmen and Marines are being placed into situations whereby they have to make split-second decisions on whether or not to use deadly force in defense of self and innocent others. Unfortunately, their decisions are often judged in the clear vision of 20-20 hindsight by political and media entities that do not know the first thing about the legal and tactical realities of a fire fight.

Because our forces have been in near-continuous combat since 2001, we possess for the first time since WWII a high percentage of the military force that has experienced combat. But in many ways we are still behaving like the risk-averse, peace time Army that pulled assignments in Germany and South Korea where one's rifle was something that stayed in the arms room and not taken out until the yearly weapons qualification. We now have a new generation of warriors that have performed as well as the much vaunted Greatest Generation of WWII, but we insist on impeding them with pre-9/11 rules. The asymmetric nature of our enemies' tactics further militates for change.

More disturbingly, these same fine young Americans are not receiving proper legal and tactical guidance from within their own services. This is the result of many problems. This book will attempt to address some of the critical legal and tactical training short-comings that need to be fixed in order to provide both legal top cover for our forces as well as provide them with the skills necessary to survive and win close quarters tactical engagements. Without providing serious and realistic recommendations for effective change, it would be one more in a series of those trendy books of late which take pot shots from the sidelines at America's armed forces. Therefore, we share some solutions: some of which have already been incorporated into training regimens throughout the joint forces.

In America, once a lawyer gets his nose under the tent flap of an organization, his corpulent body will often follow. Hence, there are more attorneys in Washington, D.C. than all of Japan. Sadly, in some respects, the military is following the lead of Washington rather than Japan. In the Army alone, their ranks have swollen to well over 1,500 uniformed attorneys.

All of this is not to say that lawyers have no place in the military: perhaps no place more so than the enforcement of discipline. Judge advocates have been justly referred to as the conscience of the Corps, enforcing not only discipline but encouraging and helping commanders follow just and lawful paths in areas as diverse as fiscal and environmental law. But in areas of operational law—specifically those areas concerning the application of deadly force and rules of engagement—they have become an unintentional catalyst of a risk-averse plague that is eroding our Nation's ability to conduct war.

Victorious command in combat requires risk-takers and decision-makers. Attorneys, in an effort to protect their "client" commanders, have created a risk-averse mentality that has bled over into the conduct of war.

How did this happen? Let us be clear in stating that, but for a few well-entrenched marplots, it was not a deliberate conspiracy by military attorneys to infect or subvert the system. In fact, most JAG officers are extremely patriotic and well-intentioned. Rather, it is the method by which most attorneys traditionally think, rationalize, and reason which should be recognized as anathema to an effective, combat ready organization that should always be prepared to use deadly force in self-defense.

A client's need for a lawyer is largely based on fear. Sometimes that fear is meritorious, as when an accused is facing jail time for an alleged criminal act. In such an instance it is prudent that a Soldier has an attorney. A fair justice system is an effective one. What has happened, however, is that the modern all-volunteer force has been transformed into a "zero defect" organization. In such an organization, a commander often needs an attorney just to successfully navigate all the perceived hazards in the course of promotion to the next rank. Hazards, interestingly enough, created mostly by the attorneys themselves. Over the course of two generations, many commanders have learned that by not rocking the boat, taking risks, or doing anything that may be perceived as off the reservation—and certainly never doing anything that might be politically incorrect or not safe—they will get promoted.

Hence in Iraq, at the time of this writing, every Soldier-involved shooting is investigated by the Army's Criminal Investigation Division (CID). That the military would charter a criminally-focused investigation into the actions and decisions of Soldiers and commanders who exercise their inherent right of self-defense in time of war is outrageous.

Things were not always so bad. There was a time not so long ago, when *esprit de corps* and a warrior mentality dominated our armed forces. Decision-making and trust had always been delegated to the lowest levels in America's armed forces, which is why we win our battles. The purpose of this book is to examine a specific area of operational law and tactical instruction—concerned with the inherent right of self-defense—where things have gone awry and to make suggestions as to what can be done to more effectively wage war as a Nation and protect our service members under the true color of law.

An operational law attorney, as a competent scrivener, can help fashion clear, concise rules on such limitations. When it comes to defining or restricting the use of force in self-defense, however, the written word is nearly useless. It is in this latter realm that lawyers, ignorant of the tactical realities of a firefight, can do the most damage. Interestingly enough, however, lawyers may hold the key for the solution. In the FBI, it was the lawyers who brought about the changes in the outlook on deadly force policy and training, not the operators. But as the FBI did, the military must first learn a new way of thinking. No one likes to be told that their long-held and often-stated views are wrong. Winston Churchill stated "I love to learn, but I do not always like being taught." We must, however, educate the lawyers and the operators to a new way of thinking in regard to deadly force policy and training.

Other than in conflicts where America's national leadership has designated a "hostile" force to be targeted at will, Soldiers, Sailors, Airmen and Marines will *always* be responding to a hostile act or demonstrated hostile intent (much as police officers do on a daily basis in the United States). Accordingly, it is extremely important that our service members are educated on threat identification. It simply does not make sense to ignore the decades of law enforcement experience in this area of both the law and tactics.

Lawyers can be "force multipliers," but only lawyers who are "switched on" to the dynamics of a tactical encounter and have the best interest of their clients (the mission and individual Soldiers, Sailors, Airmen and Marines vice *just* the Command) at heart. This book presents a lawful and reasonable approach on how commanders and judge advocates can better equip our forces in their business of killing those who would do harm to America.

CHAPTER TWO

THE PROBLEM

DESPITE A CLEAR MANDATE SET FORTH in the Chairman of the Joint Chiefs of Staff's Standing Rules of Engagement[1]—"Unit Commanders at all levels shall ensure that individuals within their respective units understand and are trained on when and how to use force in self-defense"—most Soldiers, Sailors, Airmen and Marines are not properly trained on threat recognition and the appropriate, immediate tactical response to a hostile act or demonstrated hostile intent. This creates both a heightened risk for friendly forces as well as a greater likelihood of a legally and tactically inappropriate use of force. Neither option bodes well for mission success, and as exemplified by the two following news reports from Iraq, creates constant tension and confusion at the senior leader level:

> American commanders in Iraq are taking steps intended to lessen the chance for violent confrontations between their troops and innocent Iraqis during the daily routines of operating checkpoints and running convoys, senior military officers said.
>
> The changes reflect deep worries that the conduct of American soldiers continues to alienate many Iraqis, despite three years of efforts by the American military to promote greater awareness among the troops of how their actions are perceived.
>
> The changes are meant to avoid confrontations that escalate

[1]Chairman of the Joint Chiefs of Staff Instruction (CJCSI) 3121.01B, para. 1b (13June2005)

into the use of force, for example by substituting signs or other gentler warnings for the firing of warning shots, or using strobe lights to make sure civilian drivers approaching checkpoints can see the Americans clearly.

Lt. Gen. Peter W. Chiarelli, commander of day-to-day military operations in Iraq, took the unusual step of forwarding to his two-star Army and Marine Corps commanders recent articles in the British press that condemned American forces for what were described as unnecessary levels of rough behavior.

"I don't think it hurts us at all to take a look at it, and ask some tough questions about how we're perceived and how we act as soldiers here in Iraq," General Chiarelli said in a recent telephone interview from his headquarters near Baghdad. "It falls in line with what I'm trying to do in urging a higher level of understanding and cultural sensitivity."

"What we are asking people to do is think through and talk through with soldiers the 'shoot-no shoot' scenarios, and ask, 'When should you apply deadly force?' said General Chiarelli, who in January took over the Multinational Corps-Iraq and became the second-highest-ranking American combat commander in the country. "We want to give the soldier the opportunity to make the best decision possible."

- New York Times, May 2, 2006

We face a serious strategic dilemma. Are U.S. combat troops operating in a police action governed by the rule of Iraqi law? Or are they a Coalition Military Force supporting a counter-insurgency campaign in a nation with almost no functioning institutions? The situation must remain ambiguous until the Iraqi government is actually operating effectively. We currently have excellent rules of engagement (ROE) governing the use of lethal force. These rules are now morphing under the pressures of political sensitivity at tactical level.

Many U.S. Soldiers feel constrained not to use lethal force as the option of first instance against clearly identified and armed AIF terrorists—but instead follow essentially police procedures. Without question, we must clearly and dramatically rein in the use of lethal force—and zero out the collateral killing or wounding of innocent civilians trying to survive in this war zone. However, the tactical rules of engagement will need constant monitoring to maintain an appropriate balance.

- Academic Report of General Barry R. McCaffrey, USA(Ret.) to United States Military Academy, Department of Social Sciences, April 25, 2006.

Lieutenant General Chiarelli understands that Soldiers need to be constantly drilled and rehearsed in situational training exercises on threat identification and response. And General McCaffery recognizes the almost palpable hesitancy of US forces to use lethal force when necessary, but even he, an experienced combat veteran, falls into the same trap many Judge Advocates do when he states that commands should constantly tinker with the rules governing the use of force. To the contrary, the rules should remain fairly static: "You may use deadly force if you reasonably believe yourself or innocent others to be in imminent danger of death of serious bodily injury."

Despite the following robust language in the Secretary of Defense-approved Standing Rules of Engagement (SROE)[2] that sets forth the inherent right of self-defense and provides guidance for the application of force for mission accomplishment outside the Continental United States (OCONUS):

Inherent Right of Self-Defense. Unit Commanders always retain the inherent right and obligation to exercise unit self-defense in response to a hostile act or demonstrated hostile intent. Unless otherwise directed by a unit commander as directed below, military members may exercise self-defense in response to a hostile act or demonstrated hostile intent. Para.3.a.

Or fairly clear language for our military police and security forces: "You may use force, including deadly force, when you reasonably believe yourself or others to be in imminent danger of death or serious bodily harm."- AFI 31-207 1.4.1 (Mirrored in AR 190-14)

---

[2]CJCSI 3121.01B (13June2005)

Self-imposed confusion continues to gnaw at our combat forces. This confusion flows from commanders and lawyers having a difficult time coming to terms with the following question: "What the heck constitutes hostile intent or imminent threat?"

Many commands turn to their legal advisors to draft and implement guidance concerning this area of concern. Sadly, this often results not in concise rules and better training, but rather in a plethora of ever-tightening, ever-changing and tactically ridiculous rules of engagement being forced down upon our forces. The resultant confusion and hesitation makes us a less effective force, as demonstrated by the following real-world examples:

MP Detachment Robbed at Gunpoint in Afghanistan

(Incident as reported by Provost Marshal/Force Protection Officer for a compound of approximately 300 Soldiers and several smaller compounds spread over Afghanistan with Soldiers numbering from 10 to 50 Soldiers each)

"Late one evening two Soldiers—one Staff Sergeant and one Specialist—were returning to the main compound escorting a humanitarian assistance convoy. As they were traveling down a relatively busy street a vehicle came along side of them. It was carrying two uniformed Afghan individuals; the uniforms appeared military in nature. The vehicle began to swerve back and forth then sped up and cut in front of them at an angle and forced the Soldiers to stop. The two Afghans jumped from their vehicle brandishing AK-47s. One Afghan stood in front of the soldier's vehicle with his weapon pointed at them and the other Afghan walked up to the left, driver's side of the vehicle. He pointed his weapon toward the vehicle and told the Soldiers he wanted their money. They told him they didn't have money and the Afghan became more forceful and belligerent, demonstrably pointing his weapon toward the Soldiers and telling them again to give him their money. At this time the Soldiers got their wallets, pulled out some money and gave it to the Afghan. The Afghan wasn't satisfied that he had all the money and once again he became forceful. He bent into the window with his weapon and told them he wanted it all. The Specialist gave him the rest of the money he had. The Afghan was satisfied this time because both Soldiers showed the inside of their wallets. He walked back to the car; both men got in the car and drove away. They made off with close to $200, which is a lot for a Soldier and a huge sum for an Afghani.

"The two Soldiers made their way back to the compound and reported the incident to me. Obviously, my first question was "Why didn't you shoot them?" The Soldiers replied that they were not sure this was an incident where they would have been justified in doing so. They felt that since this wasn't actual combat and they weren't fired at first they were not justified in self-defense and shooting them would have been the wrong thing to do and they would have been in trouble.

"Immediately following this incident, the JAG[3] lawyers assigned to the unit conducted a ROE class. I was thinking this was great, because now we would get all the Soldiers clear on the ROE and they would be more apt to protect themselves from something like this in the future. Unbelievably, the two lawyers told everyone the Soldiers were exactly right in the way they reacted. They stated that since the Soldiers didn't feel their lives were threatened and the Afghans had not shot at them then they didn't have justification to shoot. They also said there was no real threat and the Afghans were only robbing them, and since it wasn't an act of war, shooting them would not have been justified! So here we were back to ground zero. The conversation among the Soldiers (myself included) following this ROE class was basically this: if you don't have the right to shoot the enemy when he is threatening you with a weapon and is robbing you literally at gunpoint then when do you have the right to defend yourself? Once you're lying on the ground half dead...or worse?"

ECP Guards in the Green Zone

In January 2004, the author had the opportunity to interview five young Soldiers performing Entry Control Point (ECP) duty at the Coalition Provisional Authority Headquarters in the Green Zone in Baghdad. Each of the Soldiers, after they had gotten "off duty," was asked the musical question "When do you believe you can use deadly force?" The author received

---

[3]NOTE: Upon further inquiry, it was determined that these two lawyers were not Judge Advocates, but rather Army Civil Affairs officers, who were either former Judge Advocates or simply attorneys in their civilian careers. This is important for two reasons: Judge Advocates— not Civil Affairs officers—provide command legal guidance; and (2) the underlying message—too often repeated by real JAGs—reinforced confusion over the right to use force. This is why tactically "switched on" JAGs need to be providing legal guidance of this nature, not hand-wringers.

five different answers, including one look akin to a hog staring at a wrist watch, but the overarching theme of each young Soldier was "I don't know, Sir, but I do know that I will be in trouble if I fire my weapon." This seeking of affirmation—in other words, it is OK to shoot—is not unusual.

Insurgents Emplacing IEDs outside the Wire

(As related to one of the authors by noncommissioned officer and Operation Iraqi Freedom veteran attending an iteration of the ROE/RUF Tactical Training Seminar at Fort Knox, Kentucky in May 2005)

"We were pulling perimeter guard duty at our FOB (forward operating base), when a young squad member noticed two civilian-dressed Iraqis emplacing a 155 mm artillery shell outside the wire. This was typical insurgent TTP (tactics, techniques and procedure) for setting up an IED (improvised explosive device). The young soldier knew he should shoot these guys, but hesitated because he had heard of others getting in trouble for firing before, so he got on the radio and called his squad leader. The squad leader called the platoon leader, and before we knew it, it had made it all the way to Brigade level. There, the Brigade Commander, who wasn't even on the scene, order us not to fire and that he would send out helicopters to scout the area. A while later, two Kiowa Warriors came, fired a bunch of rockets, missed the insurgents by 30 meters, and then one of the dang things crashed on the way back to base...go figure!" The young Soldier at the squad level had all the legal, moral and tactical authority to shoot two people desperately in need of being shot, but was only seeking affirmation.

Marines at Fallujah

In Spring 2004, unclassified portions of the Rules of Engagement designated members of Iraqi insurgency groups as hostile forces that could be engaged at will. Instead of taking advantage of this authority to kill bad guys, many subordinate units—to include Marines at Fallujah—layered on overly restrictive ROE. Unbelievably, at the tactical level, one Marine unit[4] was ordered not to fire unless fired upon. In addition to being unnecessarily dangerous and tactically foolish, such guidance was contrary to the

---

[4]This information was provided to the authors by a Special Mission Unit member who witnessed the Marines' plight while his unit's sniper teams were killing insurgents by the score.

authority provided by higher headquarters. Moreover, it was in direct contravention to the Marines' inherent right of self-defense.

In a world where technology allows four-star commanders to make near real-time tactical decisions from a headquarters thousands of miles away from the conflict, the temptation to substitute their judgment for the judgment of the Soldier on the ground is very strong and prevalent. In an ironic chapter of Tommy Frank's book, *American Soldier*, he details how he and his staff, too include his Judge Advocate, Navy Captain Shelley Young, all from a headquarters thousands of miles away from the action, made the call not to launch a one-missile, tactical strike from an armed Predator on a vehicular convoy suspected of transporting Taliban leader Mullah Omar. The irony is that the same Tommy Franks, as a young lieutenant in Vietnam, bemoaned higher headquarters interfering with his ability to make tactical decisions on the field of battle. News reports right after the incident unfairly blamed Captain Young for "making the wrong call." The decision is always the Commanders', not the lawyers'. While a Predator-feed[5] launch decision may be the exception, what the news stories continually fail to appreciate is how ridiculous it is to have a four-star commander involved at all with such a tactical decision in time of war.

Former US Envoy to Iraq, Paul Bremmer's bemoaning that his mission was constantly being tinkered with by Washington's "ten thousand mile screwdriver" is a systemic problem. When that ten thousand mile screwdriver attempts to restrict a Soldier's judgment and inherent right of self-defense, however, it becomes a deadly serious systemic issue. And the more that lawyers, unskilled and unaware of the tactical dynamics of a deadly force encounter, attempt to substitute their judgment for the Soldiers' via restrictive and tactically absurd ROE guidance, the more deadly the problem becomes.

---

[5]On certain occasions, there are no tactical operators on the ground to give direction or make the call for the employment of such a weapon system. In this case the call—whether or not to launch a Hellfire missile from an armed Predator unmanned aerial vehicle—would be made from a remote headquarters.

CHAPTER 3

THE PROBLEM AND
WHY IT EXISTS?
FEAR OF FORCE

PRIOR TO SEPTEMBER 11, 2001, an Infantry Battalion Commander lecturing at the Army's Judge Advocate General's School after a "successful" tour in Bosnia once described his mission as a success because his troops didn't have to fire a shot. This is a dangerous definition of mission success, as the mission—whether it is handing out beans in Guatemala or full, force on force conflict—is what it is. Its success should never be judged by whether one has to use force, especially in self-defense.

It is exactly this fear of using force that resulted in a paratrooper from the 82nd Airborne Division losing an eye after being attacked by two-by-four wielding thugs in Kosovo: the trooper either didn't understand that such thugs presented an imminent threat of death or serious bodily injury or was improperly briefed on his right to use force in self-defense. The paratrooper never knew that it would have been OK to shoot the bastards in self-defense. The Army then added insult to injury by awarding medals for the show of restraint!

Strangely, this over cautiousness when it comes to using force is not rooted in the law. To the contrary, the law supports a robust and vigorous response, especially in the areas of self-defense. Its robust nature will be explored in depth in later chapters, but even such a seemingly pacifistic document as the United Nations Charter recognizes this inherent right.

Synthesized down to its essence, Article 51 of the UN Charter states that any offensive (legally, not tactically speaking) use of force is unlawful and any defensive (so long as proportional in the law of armed conflict sense) use of force is lawful. On a nation-state scale, the unprovoked invasion of one sovereign nation by another is unlawful, as is, on an individual scale, the unprovoked assault and battery of one person by another. Both the aggrieved nation state and the individual victim may use reasonable force to defend themselves, to wit: Kuwait's violent eviction of Iraq in 1991, as well as any citizen's use of force to defend themselves from the thugs of society.

Somehow, these simple principles have been lost when it comes to teaching our warriors threat identification and response. The root of the problem comes from a profound misunderstanding by judge advocates and commanders as to the rules concerning the use of force, the tactical dynamics surrounding a use of force situation, as well as two collateral issues: unclear command guidance and "accidental" discharge (AD) paranoia.

Generally, weapon systems do not "accidentally" discharge. They discharge when the operator inserts trigger finger in trigger housing group at an inopportune moment. It is remedied by proper training, not by the institution of stupid rules. By way of example of stupid rules: In March 2003, I was in Camp Doha, Kuwait providing ROE/RUF training to members of SEAL Team 3 and 5th Special Forces Group just prior to the start of Operation IRAQI FREEDOM. Despite the fact that there was a real, high-risk terrorist threat in and around Kuwait City at the time (two civilian contractors were brutally murdered in cold blood by a terrorist ambush), CFLCC (Combined Forces Land Component Command) ROE specified that if Soldiers, Sailors, Airmen or Marines left Camp Doha (in Kuwait City), they had to be "two up per vehicle, two vehicles per convoy, seat-belted in, and wearing ballistic body armor" but they were not to load a round into the chamber of their weapons unless confronted with a "hostile act." Thank God, the author was assigned to CFSOCC (Combined

Forces Special Operations Component Command), and didn't have to abide by such nonsensical rules, but the fact remains that whoever authored and promulgated such idiocies was more concerned about answering the mail for an "AD" than providing adequate and reasonable defenses for his forces. Moreover, the practice of imposing field grade nonjudicial punishment on individuals who suffer an accidental discharge instills an unreasonable fear of weapons. Lastly, such punishment is unjust if not accompanied by proper weapons training.

Fear of Weapons

A philosophical sea change has occurred over the past four decades concerning attitudes towards weapons and weapons systems. Two generation's worth of exposure to Disney's vilification of firearms has turned America from a nation that respects and relies on firearms to one that views weapons as either intrinsically evil or, at best, instrumentalities to be feared.

For an entity that calls itself "the Armed Forces," most service members—perhaps with the exception of the Marines—never initially develop an intimate and close relationship with firearms. Often to the contrary, service members are taught to fear rather than become masters of their individual weapons. Such fearful attitudes, often the result of Hollywood and media-engendered perceptions concerning firearms, are reinforced by first-time experiences at Basic Military Training ranges. There, and often throughout one's career, service members are exposed to well-intentioned but misguided leaders that are too focused on "safety" rather than true familiarization and development of tactically useful foundational skill sets. For example, no one can logically explain why, after Soldiers are taught to properly clear and safe a weapon, too include visually and manually inspecting the chamber, an NCO "rods" people off a range. Not only does this practice of ramming a steel rod from the muzzle end of a rifle into the face of the bolt carrier group foster a sense of mistrust and fear of the weapon, but it also subjects the crown, rifling and bolt face of the weapon to unnecessary abuse. Experienced tactical training instructors often spend hours assisting students in overcoming this learned fear.

Misunderstanding the TacticalDynamics
of a Deadly Force Encounter

Most deadly force encounters occur under situations that "are tense, uncertain, and rapidly evolving," and the good guys are nearly always behind the action-reaction power curve. Add to this unhealthy and dangerous mix the fact that the human mind's ability to think clearly and the body's ability to react quickly is seriously degraded due to the stress of high-threat events, and we often have a recipe for bad results. As discussed in later chapters, one must gain an understanding of these tactical dynamics before offering effective training or drafting rules impacting the application of force. Sadly, most commanders and their lawyers—even ones with so-called combat arms experience—are woefully ignorant of these matters.

Misunderstanding the Laws Concerning the Use of Force

Any competent judge advocate will go to the ends of the earth to discover relevant and powerful law to back the positions of their client. In criminal cases, for instance, first term judge advocates will diligently research "case law" to find legal precedent in their client's favor. Environmental or fiscal law attorneys will scour regulatory guidance and opinions to find "the right" answer for their client's position. In every other area of the law except operational law, lawyers are encouraged to do this. In operational law settings, however, most lawyers remain ignorant of a huge body of Federal and state law extant concerning the reasonableness of the use of deadly force in self-defense. Instead, they are satisfied by cutting and pasting legally unsupportable and tactically inefficient "ROE' from diverse websites, to include the Army's Center for Law and Military Operations (CLAMO). When any voice of opposition or reason is raised, they are quickly shouted down or pooh-poohed by those few "intellectuals" who are either defending their rice bowls or ignorant of the tactical realities faced by their clients: the end-users of such guidance.

Bottom line: the law provides extraordinary leeway and protection for the good guys' decisions to use force in self-defense. Unfortunately, the risk-averse set of lawyers has obfuscated this fact from their clients, instead substituting their own ill-conceived and ignorant notions of what constitutes reasonable use of force. This unnecessarily and irresponsibly endangers our young men and women in the line of fire.

Unclear Command Guidance

Many times, Soldiers (as do law enforcement officers), even when they recognize and are confronted with an imminent threat of death or serious bodily injury, will not pull the trigger for fear that they will "get in trouble" for their actions under a post-mortem review. In the scenario set forth above concerning the sentry spotting the insurgents emplacing an IED, the Soldier was merely looking for affirmation of his righteous decision to shoot. Unfortunately, such affirmation was not forthcoming. The SROE is very clear in enunciating the right and obligation to exercise self-defense. By the time this strategic guidance reaches the end-user—the kid on the pointy end of the spear—it has been tinkered with and watered down by sometimes well meaning commanders and judge advocates that it is nearly unrecognizable.

In the FBI, then-Director Louis Freeh recognized this problem and incorporated into FBI policy language right out of case law: "If an FBI Agent uses deadly force in self-defense, he or she will not be judged in the clear vision of 20-20 hindsight, but rather how a reasonable Agent would act under circumstances that are tense uncertain and rapidly evolving."

Fortunately, many commanders are turning to similar guidance for their Soldiers, as exemplified by both MG Webster's guidance and MG Harrell's guidance to 3rd Infantry Division and Special Operations Command Central members, respectively, during Operation Iraqi Freedom. Absent such guidance, Soldiers are left to wonder whether the command will stand behind them if they make a decision to shoot. In both General Webster's and General Harrell's tours of command in Iraq, they were confronted with situations where some of their Soldiers were involved in initially "questionable"[6] shooting incidents. Both General Harrell and

---

[6]In January 2005, 3rd Infantry Division Soldiers manning a traffic control point (TCP) on the highway leading from downtown Baghdad to Baghdad International Airport (BIAP) engaged a vehicle that failed to slow down when approaching the TCP. Unfortunately, due to a series of miscommunications, the vehicle contained a recently released Italian journalist and her rescuer, an Italian intelligence officer. The Italian intelligence officer was killed.

In May 2003, a Special Forces officer shot and killed an apparently "unarmed" Iraqi who was operating the lead vehicle in a group of civilian vehicles setting up an apparent vehicular ambush on the convoy the Special Forces officer was charged with protecting. In the initial message traffic immediately following the incident, General Harrell's headquarters was queried with "Why are SF members shooting unarmed Iraqis in an act of road rage?" Not unlike how many reporters and civil rights groups—unschooled in the realities of threat recognition—might react to an incident in any major metropolis in America. A more detailed account of this incidence can be found in the June 6, 2005 edition of *Army Times* in a story by Sean Naylor.

General Webster had the intestinal fortitude and honor to stand by their word and support their Soldiers. In light of some of the legal guidance put out by some other commands, one is left to wonder whether such command support would be forthcoming. Soldiers, rightly or wrongly, perceive that overly restrictive written ROE will merely be used either as a shield for the command or a sword to come after the Soldiers post-incident.

"Accidental" Discharge Paranoia

There is generally no such thing as an "accidental" discharge. Normally weapons do not fire accidentally. Rather, they go off when an operator inserts his or her trigger finger into the trigger housing group and depresses (perhaps inadvertently) the trigger. Nevertheless, instead of taking the relatively short amount of training time to properly instruct troops on trigger finger and muzzle discipline, in turn greatly reducing the likelihood of such an occurrence, commanders are so paranoid of "accidental" discharges that they set up "clearing barrels" all over their compounds and impose inane rules on when and where a Soldier may load a round into the chamber. These restrictions can have deadly implications on a Soldier's ability to place his weapon into action if and when confronted with an imminent threat.

Also, there is a disturbing tendency amongst lawyers to label every unintentional discharge of a weapon as a "negligent" discharge. We are making a legal conclusion every time we use the phrase, and thus it should only be used in situations where guilt and negligence has been proven. Just like vehicle accidents, or the use of paring knives in the kitchen, some degree of accident is to be expected as the price of doing business. But, not all such incidents are the result of negligence. When we get to the point that we treat unintentional discharges like vehicle accidents, then we will have come a long way.

CHAPTER 4

MISUNDERSTANDING OF RULES GOVERNING USE OF DEADLY FORCE (OVER-LAWYERING THE ISSUE)

WHEN WE SEND FINE YOUNG AMERICANS into harm's way, we have a moral and legal obligation to provide them with Rules of Engagement (ROE) that protect their right of self-defense to the maximum extent possible under the mission parameters. It would be an understatement to say that confusion exists among commanders and judge advocates as to what constitutes a reasonable use of deadly force by U.S. forces and when that force is authorized.

As discussed in the succeeding few chapters, International Law, as well as the Constitutional and common law of the United States, provides ample support for the establishment of vigorous guidelines concerning the use of deadly force. Every relevant legal system in the free world makes aggression a crime and protects the right of self-defense. This right is often referred to as an "inherent right" or a "divine right." Judge advocates and commanders crafting rules of engagement have too often ignored this rich source of law favorable to a vigorous defensive posture.

One of the first mistakes a judge advocate can make when providing legal advice in this area of the law is to view their role as the "commander's lawyer." In other words, look for ways to insulate the commander from future legal scrutiny. In most areas of the law, such an approach would be considered prudent. For instance, when dealing with environmental law concerns, it would be wise to advise the command to stay one step to the rear and one step to the right of whatever proscription exist concerning the disposal of hazardous material. Or, to keep a commander out of trouble, it may behoove a judge advocate to craft command policies that fall well within the current state of the law boundaries concerning sexual harassment. This is all good, preventive lawyering. It does not work, however, when one is in the realm of the laws surrounding the use of deadly force in self-defense. The law allows a *reasonable* use of force, and it makes no sense legally or tactically to change that to a *minimum* use of force or to add *last resort* or *exhaust* all lesser means language. Yet, this is exactly what is being done across the mission spectrum from Iraq to relief operations such as Hurricane Katrina, unnecessarily endangering the lives of our forces.

Incorporation of Constitutional and common law into the development of enhanced force protection and self-defense rules in the military will only enhance our forces' ability to accomplish their missions. From humanitarian assistance to force-on-force conflicts, if potential opponents believe our forces are vulnerable to attack, the mission is compromised. Further, International Law is shaped by the infusion of diverse legal concepts from around the world. Why not shape it by infusing American principles?

Recurrent, hands-on tactical exercises provide service members an opportunity to viscerally experience the psychological and physiological dynamics of a tactical encounter. Those so trained, however, need clear and concise legal guidance reinforcing that both legal and political support is present if deadly force is used.

The SROE states that commanders "have the obligation to ensure that individuals within their respective units understand and are trained on when and how to use force in self-defense." As demonstrated by the confusion at the tactical level, this obligation is not being met. On the legal and political front, clear and supportive guidance would give American military personnel—those who actually have to apply deadly force—the critical tools necessary to do that job correctly and protect themselves from the potential adverse consequences associated with an improper use of deadly force. Unfortunately, the DoD has seemingly ignored both Federal common law and Constitutional decisions concerning the use of deadly force in its development of the SROE as well as tactical-level ROE. There may be situations in which a Soldier, Sailor, Airman, or Marine may be constrained by policy not to fire on an otherwise dangerous subject[7]. Such situations, however, should be the tactical exception rather than the rule, and should be solely within the unfettered purview of leaders at the absolute lowest levels. Moreover, the constraining policy imposed should not result in an unnecessary risk to the service member. This is not, as some suggest, a usurpation of military authority[8]. It should be remembered that military leaders have the authority to order subordinates to "take that hill," but not the right to order them to charge with fixed bayonets when machine guns are available.

Yet another concern is the availability of cover: deadly force may still be necessary where the felon can find or is seeking tactical cover. A dangerous individual can represent a continuing threat, despite the seemingly non-threatening actions of a subject fleeing the scene. That is why blanket proscriptions, as seen on many modern ROE cards, on a Soldier's ability to fire on fleeing subjects makes no sense tactically or legally.

Once an individual has made the decision to open fire, the next question is for how long can he continue to fire? Again, in contrast to many admonitions contained in modern examples of ROE, a Federal agent is not required to "shoot and assess" or "use minimum force." Instead, one should apply force until the threat is over: either the subject surrenders or no longer poses an imminent threat. This determination, rather than the number of rounds fired, is a more accurate measure of reasonableness. Further, under the stressful conditions of a deadly force encounter, it is unrealistic and tactically unsound to require the counting of rounds.

When confronted with the proposal of adding a deadly force policy and training that is similar to the law enforcement's, many have voiced a concern that this will impair our warfighting capability by causing young troops to

---

[7] Public discussion generated at the XVIII Airborne Corps' Joint Rules of Engagement Conference, Fort Bragg, North Carolina, May 17-18, 2001.

[8] E.g., if an armed subject is hiding among a crowd of unarmed noncombatants, or if to return fire would provoke a more dangerous response. Just as in civilian law enforcement settings, the *authority* to fire does not mean a service member *must* fire.

hesitate when ordered to fire at a declared combatant in a traditional force on force environment. This argument is without merit for two reasons: First, it assumes that personnel are incapable of following orders to switch from one rule to another (an assumption belied by both practical experience and the routine use of phased ROEs in battle planning). Secondly, the alternative as it now stands—commanders prohibiting individuals to lock and load magazines for fear of unintended discharges or, as happens throughout the theater, sending Army CID personnel to investigate every discharge of a firearm—in no way can be viewed as inculcating a warrior mentality.

There will always be an inherent tension between operators and policy makers. Too often, just as in law enforcement bureaucracies, policy makers are more concerned about liability and not enough about survivability. Uniformed judge advocates, however, should concern themselves with enhancing our commands' survivability within the parameters of the law, not with helping risk-averse commanders play CYA.

CHAPTER 5

SINCE THE SHEEPDOG PROTECTS THE HERD, THE LAW PROTECTS THE SHEEPDOG! NATURAL LAW AND THE INHERENT RIGHT OF SELF-DEFENSE

WE ARE A NATION OF LAWS. Laws exist for a reason: there is perhaps no more important distinction that separates American forces' killing in combat from the wanton killing of many of our adversaries than America's adherence to this rule of law. Individuals look to the law to know what is and is not permissible conduct. In most cases, the law is clear. You can consume alcohol if you are twenty-one years old or older. You cannot rob a bank. The underlying problem concerning the law as it pertains to the application of deadly force in self-defense is that it is not capable of such precise definition. This is because one cannot accurately predict the factual circumstances that may give rise to a law enforcement or defensive interaction.

In most cases where one needs legal interpretation they have the luxury of time to consult with an attorney to gain an understanding of an otherwise unclear law. Unfortunately, in most deadly force encounters, failure to act right now gets you killed and you don't have time to put the world on hold and dial 1-800-LAWYER. In these circumstances we look to examples where a court examined and applied the law to some set of facts, and then apply the courts' conclusion and reasoning to the future situations we may face. It is imperative that the standard be simple, easily understood, and easily applied in situations where seconds count and mistakes cost lives.

To provide guidance, Agencies and Departments take the judicial standard and draft policy and rules-based documents instructing its employees on how to apply the law. In most instances, by the time the court's reasoning filters its way through the lawyers, the end iteration is typically anything but simple, easily understood, or easily applied.

This is not to say that policies and rules do not serve an important purpose. When properly drafted, policy serves the vital role of taking a generic standard of law and tailoring it to a specific mission or focus. Problems arise when lawyers draft policies that improperly or too narrowly interpret a judicial standard, thus adding yet one more layer of confusion between the original standard of law and the end user. The purpose of this section is to tear down the layers of confusion and get right to the heart of the matter: the pure law of when one can and cannot use deadly force in self-defense.

Consistently, since at least 60 B.C. , individuals have had an inherent right to reasonably defend themselves from an attacker threatening to inflict death or serious bodily injury. Modern law does not abrogate this God-given universal right; it merely provides guidance on what constitutes reasonableness to do so.

Recognizing the need for policy and rules, we must also recognize that we owe it to Soldiers who voluntarily place themselves in harms' way to provide them with rules and policy protecting their right to life to the maximum extent possible under the mission parameters. We provide Soldiers with the finest gear and equipment, so it follows that we must provide them with the finest Rules of Engagement (ROE) to give them best opportunity to successfully complete their mission and safely return home. ROE serve as written rules governing weapons systems, geography, time and space, and authority for release. ROE are not intended to serve as a play-by-play guidebook for hostile interactions. It is very rare (.01% of military engagements) when our civilian leadership designates a hostile combatant, thus authorizing Soldiers to engage the enemy at will without responding to a hostile act or demonstration of hostile intent. Even in such limited cases, the enemy we face no longer wears a uniform with a clear enemy "team" patch on the sleeve. Al-Qaeda doesn't wear monogrammed t-shirts. By default then our forces must quickly and accurately respond defensively to a hostile act or demonstration of hostile intent.

In the same way domestic law enforcement officers respond to the actions of a suspect they're in contact with, our troops must learn to observe enemy actions and respond in accordance with their training and experience. When a law enforcement officer uses deadly force in the line of duty, the officer's actions and decisions will not be second-guessed as long as the act was "objectively reasonable." Based on the particular facts and circumstances the officer faced at the moment deadly force was implemented, and recognizing the fact that officers must make critical decisions in a split second, an officer's actions are judged based on whether no reasonable officer could have believed the facts and circumstances at that moment justified that action. If yes, the inquiry goes no further, case closed, go back to your beat; the act was justified. The same should hold true for our Soldiers serving overseas. They face the same split second decision making processes and require specialized training and expertise to perform their job, and Soldiers rarely face the same factual scenario more than once. Therefore it is appropriate that Soldiers' use of deadly force be examined under the same reasonableness standard applied to domestic law enforcement.

As demonstrated below, the inherent right of self-defense is a natural, Divine right, and cannot be abrogated by law or custom. In drafting the U.S. Constitution, the Founding Fathers looked to English Common law, which uniformly recognized individual's inherent right to self-defense. People's inherent right of self-defense pre-existed the Constitution, and the drafters wrote of individual's right to life with the knowledge that the derivative right to defend life was fundamental. U.S. common law consistently recognizes self-defense as a defense to criminal charges of manslaughter or homicide. Under the common law, one is justified in using deadly force to repel a threat of serious bodily injury or death without first retreating or exhausting non-lethal means of repelling the attack. What is amazing—moreover frustrating—is that so-called International and Operational Law attorneys in the military routinely ignore this extensive body of law when drafting rules of engagement for our forces operating both OCONUS and CONUS.

Inherent Right of Self-Defense: Derived From Nature, Not Law

The right of self-defense arises out of a normative relationship between the defender of the right and the end that he or she is seeking to protect—one's right not to be killed by an unprovoked attack. A derivative of that right is the right of self-defense; to protect one's self from intentional, offensive deprivation of their fundamental right to life. This is commonly referred to as one's "inherent right of self-defense," and it cannot be abrogated by law, policy, or creed.

Historically, the right of self-defense has been viewed not as a statutory or legal right, but as a divine natural right permanently bestowed upon all persons by virtue of existence. Over 2,000 years ago Markus Tullius Cicero wrote:

> [t]here does exist therefore, gentlemen, a law which is a law not of the statute-book, but of nature; a law which we possess not by instruction, tradition,or reading, but which we have caught, imbided, and sucked in at Nature's ownbreast; a law which comes to us not by education but by constitution, not by training but by intuition—the law, I mean, that should our life have fallen into any snare, into the violence and the weapons of robbers or foes, every method of winning a way to safety would be morally justifiable.[9]

In 529 CE, the Roman scholar Justinian observed, "that which someone does for the safety of his body, let it be regarded as having been done legally."[10] The Old Testament provides, "If a thief be found breaking up, and be smitten that he die, there shall be no blood shed for him. If the sun be risen upon him, there shall be blood shed for him."[11]

The right of self-defense in criminal law is one deeply rooted in the legal traditions of England, the source of most American common law. The

[9]Markus Tullius Cicero, *Cicero: On Behalf of Milo*, 60 BCE.
[10]Justinian: *Digest of Roman Law*, 529 CE.
[11]Ex. 22:2-3.

right of self-defense was expressed in the statutes of King Henry VIII,[12] as a complete defense to civil and criminal prosecutions. William Blackstone, the father of English Common law,[13] wrote, "[s]elf defense is justly called the primary law of nature, so it is not, neither can it be in fact, taken away by the laws of society."[14] "The right of having and using arms for self-preservation and defense" is one of the five auxiliary rights people possess to "protect and maintain 'the three great and primary rights' personal security, personal liberty, and private property."[15] Blackstone also taught:

> All homicide is malicious, and of course, amounts to murder, unless justified by the command or permission of the law; excused on the account of accident or self-preservation; or alleviated into manslaughter, by being either the involuntary consequence of some act not strictly lawful, or (if voluntary) occasioned by some sudden and sufficiently violent provocation.[16]

Sir Michael Foster observed in the Crown Cases,

> [t]he right of self-defence [sic] in these cases is founded in the law of nature, and is not, nor can be, superseded by any law of society. For before societies were formed for mutual defence [sic] and preservation, the right of self-defence [sic] resided in individuals; it could not reside elsewhere, and since in cases of necessity, individuals incorporated into society cannot resort for protection to the law of society, that law with great propriety and strict justice considereth them, as still, in that instance, under the protection of the law of nature.[17]

To Foster, an individual's right to self-defense was a personal right and an individual retained that right even when society provided protective services intended to prevent the need for self-help through exercising self-defense. Foster touched on a topic still litigated today[18]- individuals

---

[12]24 Hen. 8, ch.5 (1532) (Eng.).

[13]Charles L. Cantrell, *the Right to Bear Arms: A Reply*, 53 Wis. B. Bull. 21-26 (Oct. 1980).

[14]3 WILLIAM BLACKSTONE, COMMENTARIES *1.

[15]William Blackstone, *Commentaries on the Laws of England*, at 141 (1766).

[16]4 W. BLACKSTONE, COMMENTARIES 201 (1854).

[17]Sir Michael Foster, *Crown Cases*, 273-274 (London 1776).

[18]See, Turner v. United States, 248 U.S. 354, 357-58 (1919), (fundamental principle that a government and its agents are under no general duty to provide public services, such as police protection, to any particular individual citizen); *see also*, Warren v. District of Columbia, 444 A.2d 1 (D.C. 1981).

must not rely on government organizations (law enforcement, military, public service agencies) to protect them from outside harm. Those services exist for the benefit of the whole rather than the specific protection of one. In emergency situations where a societal service is unavailable, individuals must be permitted, prepared, and ready to defend their own life. A former Special Forces operator coined the phrase, "you're dead until you save your own life." Even the most noble intentioned law enforcement agency cannot stand beside each member it serves to protect and keep him from harm. You're dead until you save your own life, and it might be that you have to take the life of another to keep him from taking yours.

English philosopher John Locke observed, "self defense is a part of the law or nature, nor can it be denied the community, even against the king himself"[19] In his treatise on civil government, self-defense is fundamental to the very existence of mankind. Much like one is justified in killing a wild animal if it displayed intent to attack; one is justified in taking the life of another person if that person displayed intent to do harm to you. Locke reasoned:

> it being reasonable and just, I should have a right to destroy that which threatens me with destruction: for, by the fundamental law of nature, man being to be preserved as much as possible, when all cannot be preserved, the safety of the innocent is to be preferred: and one may destroy a man who makes war upon him, or has discovered an enmity to his being, for the same reason that he may kill a wolf or a lion; because such men are not under the ties of the common law of reason, have no other rule, but that of force and violence, and so may be treated as beasts of prey, those dangerous and noxious creatures, that will be sure to destroy him whenever he falls into their power.[20]

Like Locke, St. Thomas Acquinas believed self-defense derived from natural law, but defined self-defense not based on the assailant's act, but the defender's intent. He reasoned that one acts in self-defense where his intent is not to cause harm, but to preserve his own life. The other person may be

---

[19]John Locke, *Two Treatises of Government*, 1689.
[20]John Locke, *Treatise on Government*, Chapter 3 "The State of War" §16.

harmed, but that is a product of the innocent defender's intent, which was to prevent the attacker from causing him harm.

> [K]illing one's assailant is justified, provided one does not intend to kill him. Nothing hinders one act from having two effects, only one of which is intended, while the other is beside the intention. Accordingly, the act of self-defense may have two effects; one, the saving of one's life; the other, the slaying of the aggressor. Therefore, this act, since one's intention is to save one's own life, is not unlawful, seeing that is natural to everything to keep itself in being as far as possible."[21]

While the definition of what constitutes self-defense has varied slightly, the underlying concept that individuals have a fundamental right to self-defense has not. The inherent right of self-defense pre-exists all legal documents American or otherwise. No legal document can abrogate a fundamental right and no legal document can limit your ability to defend a fundamental right, as fundamental rights trump all government created rights and obligations.

We the People!
Our American system of government is based upon enumerated rights and responsibilities set forth in the U.S. Constitution. To the Founding Fathers, the right to self-defense was not only constitutional, but pre-existed the Constitution. They believed it was an inherent, natural right that no man could take away. Self-defense sits at the heart of the rights protected by the Constitution- the right to life.

To understand the Constitution, and what the authors intended, Thomas Jefferson said "[o]n every question of construction [of the Constitution] let us carry ourselves back to the time when the Constitution was adopted, recollect the spirit manifested in the debates, and instead of trying what meaning may be squeezed out of the text, or invent against it, conform to the probable one in which it was passed."[22]

The Founding Fathers used English common law as a platform to build the U.S. Constitution. English common law long recognized individual's

---

[21]St. Thomas Acquinas, *Summa Theologica II-II,* Q. 64, art. 7 (13th century).
[22]Thomas Jefferson, in a letter to William Johnson, June 12, 1823.

right to self-defense as a natural and divine right.[23] The drafters were heavily influenced by the works of William Blackstone, and drafted the core of the Constitution to protect life, liberty and property. In Blackstone's *Commentaries on the Laws of England*, Blackstone held that the three primary rights protected by English law were the rights of personal security, personal liberty, and private property. Self-defense was a part of the right to personal security, as one could not be secure in their safety without the right to defend against those wishing to deprive him of it.[24] Mirroring Blackstone's statements, Samuel Adams wrote: "[a]mong the natural rights of the Colonists are these: First, a right to life; Secondly, to liberty; Thirdly, to property; together with the right to support and defend them in the best manner they can."[25] The Constitution reflects Blackstone's influence in the Bill of Rights, which explicitly protects individuals' rights to life, liberty, and property, and freedom from government intrusion therein.

Also in the Bill of Rights is an explicit ratification of citizen's right to use firearms in self-defense.[26] In defending the Second Amendment after ratification of the Constitution, John Adams wrote: "[t]o suppose arms in the hands of citizens, to be used at individual discretion, except in private self-defense, is a dissolution of the government"[27] Patrick Henry wrote, "Where is the difference between having our arms in possession and under our direction, and having them under the management of Congress? If our defense be the real object of having those arms, in whose hands can they be trusted with propriety, or equal safety to us, as in our own hands?"[28]

Alexander Hamilton was a prolific writer during the Constitutional Convention. In Federalist Paper #28, Hamilton wrote that citizen's inherent rights must be preserved and cannot be abrogated by the Constitution. He was concerned that should elected government officials abrogate a right enumerated in the Constitution, or otherwise refuse to recognize an

---

[23]1 Hawkins, Pleas of the Crown, Ch. 28, §14 (7th ed. 1795).

[24]William Blackstone, *Commentaries on the Laws of England*, at 141 (1766).

[25]Samuel Adams, *The Rights of Colonists*, November 20, 1772.

[26]*See* U.S. CONST. amend II; *see also* Ronald S. Resnick, *Private Arms as the Palladium of Liberty: The Meaning of the Second Amendment*, 77 U. Det. Mercy L. Rev. 1, 14 n.27 (1999) (citing several of the Founding Fathers for their view that the Second Amendment stands for the right to private self-defense).

[27]John Adams, *A Defense of the Constitution of the Government of the United States of America*, 1788.

[28]Patrick Henry, 3 J. Elliot, Debates in the Several State Conventions 45, 2d Ed. Philadelphia, 1836.

enumerated right, citizens must have recourse. Citizens must be able to call upon their inherent right of self defense, which exists notwithstanding a mandate from a governing body. He wrote, "if the representatives of the people betray their constituents, there is then no recourse left but in the exertion of that original right of self-defense which is paramount to all positive forms of government."[29]

The inherent right of self-defense has been a tenet of American law since its beginning,[30] and it has been perpetuated throughout the case law history. The Second Amendment of the Constitution recognizes individual's inherent right of self-defense, in authorizing citizens to "keep and bear arms." Historian Joyce Lee Malcolm wrote, "The Second Amendment was meant to accomplish two distinct goals, each perceived as crucial to the maintenance of liberty. First, it was meant to guarantee the individuals' right to have arms for self-defense. The second and related objective concerned the militia: The clause concerning the militia was not intended to limit ownership of arms to militia members."[31] The inherent right of self-defense was never intended to apply only to members of organized militia or law enforcement organizations. Regarding American citizens right to self-defense, *New Orleans &Northeastern Railroad Co. v. Jopes*,[32] stood for the idea that "the rules which determine what is self-defence [sic] are of universal application, and are not [diminished] by the character of the employment in which the [shooter] is engaged." Further, the common law did limit the right to self-defense or call upon a man to flee rather than fight to defend himself, as illustrated in the case of *Beard v. United States*.[33] in *Beard*, the court stated:

> [I]f the accused…had at the time reasonable grounds to believe
> and in good faith believed, that the deceased intended to take his

---

[29]Alexander Hamilton, Federalist Paper #28.

[30]See U.S. Const. amend II; see also Ronald S. Resnick, Private Arms as the Palladium of Liberty: The Meaning of the Second Amendment, 77 U. Det. Mercy L. Rev. 1, 14 n.27 (1999) (citing several of the Founding Fathers for their view that the Second Amendment stands for the right to private self-defense).

[31] Joyce Lee Malcolm, TO KEEP AND BEAR ARMS: THE ORIGINS OF AN ANGLO-AMERICAN RIGHT, 134, 162-63 (1994).

[32]142 U.S. 18 (1891) (noting that the plaintiff, a passenger on the train, was shot and injured when he approached and threatened the conductor by wielding an open knife).

[33]158 U.S. 550, 563-64 (1895) (noting that the plaintiff's land was trespassed by three armed men who sought to steal a cow and take plaintiff's life, and in an attempt to protect himself, the plaintiff struck one man across his head with his rifle, causing a mortal wound).

life or do him great bodily harm, *he was not obliged to retreat, nor to consider whether he could safely retreat, but was entitled to stand his ground* and meet any attack made upon him with a deadly weapon, in such a way and with such force as, under all the circumstances, he, at the moment, honestly believed, and had reasonable grounds to believe, was necessary to save his own life or to protect himself from great bodily injury.

In *United States v. Peterson,*[34] The D.C. Court of Appeals traced an individual's right to self-defense to William Blackstone, and held:

Self-defense, as a doctrine legally exonerating the taking of human life, is as viable now as it was in Blackstone's time, and in the case before us the doctrine is invoked in its purest form. But the law of self-defense is a law of necessity; the right of self-defense arises only when the necessity begins, and equally ends with the necessity; and never must the necessity be greater than when the force employed defensively is deadly. The necessity must bear all semblance of reality, and appear to admit of no other alternative, before taking life will be justifiable as excusable. Hinged on the exigencies of self-preservation, the doctrine of homicidal self-defense emerges from the body of the criminal law as a limited though important exception to legal outlawry of the arena of self-help in the settlement of potentially fatal personal conflicts.[35]

In *Brown v. United States,*[36] the U.S. Supreme Court affirmed the common law recognition of an inherent right of self-defense. There, the Court held:

In order to excuse or to justify the taking of human life, it must appear that the killing was reasonably necessary to protect other interests which for good reasons the law regards as more important, under all the circumstances, than the continued existence of the life in question. The difficulty lies in defining such "other interests." In so far as self-defense is concerned, the normal case of another interest is the life of a person other than the one killed. If the protection

---

[34] 483 F.2d 1222 (D.C. App. 1973).
[35] Id. at 1236, *internal citations omitted.*
[36] 256 U.S. 235 (1921).

of that life makes necessary the homicide in question, there can be no doubt that the law must excuse or justify the killing.

In affirming the doctrine of self-defense, the Court held:

Detached reflection cannot be demanded in the presence of an uplifted knife. Therefore in this Court, at least, it is not a condition of immunity that one in that situation should pause to consider whether a reasonable man might not think it possible to fly with safety or to disable his assailant [or to consider other alternatives,] rather than to kill him.[38]

Brown establishes that the common law does not require one to delay in considering non-lethal responses to an immediate threat of deadly force. If an individual is faced with a threat of death or serious bodily injury, it is necessary that the individual employ deadly force to repel the attack.

---

[38]*Id.* at 343; *see also Silas v. Bowen*, 277 F. Supp. 314, 318 (D. S.C. 1967) (stating that use of deadly weapon as self-defense is justified if a reasonable person would anticipate serious bodily harm); *United States v. Peterson*, 483 F.2d 1222, 1236 (D.C. App. 1973) (recognizing that there is no duty to retreat from an assault producing imminent danger); *Glashen v. Godshall*, 1999 U.S. Dist. LEXIS 17698, *6 (S.D.N.Y. Nov. 16, 1999); *Marche' v. Parrachak*, 2000 U.S. Dist. LEXIS 14804, *13 (E.D. Pa. Oct. 10, 2000); *United States v. Yabut*, 43 C.M.R. 233, 234 (CMA 1971).

CHAPTER 6

RIGHTS WITHOUT BORDERS: INTERNATIONAL LAW AND THE INDIVIDUAL RIGHT TO SELF-DEFENSE

CUSTOMARY AND STATUTORY INTERNATIONAL LAW recognizes individual's inherent right of self-defense. The application of anticipatory or pre-emptive self-defense and the maxim of a person's inherent right to self-defense were firmly established in the *Caroline* incident. In 1837, the British were fighting a counter-insurgency war along the Niagara River in Canada. The steamer *Caroline* was being used by the insurgents on both the American and British sides of the river. On the evening of December 29, 1837, British combatants crossed onto the American side of the river and destroyed the Caroline while it was docked in Schlosser, New York. The Americans protested, but the British responded that they were merely exercising their inherent right of self-defense. American Secretary of State Daniel Webster disagreed. In response to Lord Ashburton's claim that the British acted in self-defense, Webster declared that for an act to be self-defense, it "must be a necessity of self-defense, instant, overwhelming, leaving no choice of means and no moment for deliberation."[40] Secondly, to be appropriate, self-defense must be proportional, not "unreasonable or

---

[40]Letter from Daniel Webster, Secretary of State, to Henry Fox, British Minister in Washington, April 24, 1841.

excessive."[41] While never admitting culpability for the *Caroline* incident, the British apologized to the United States for the incident.[42]

The *Caroline* incident is the first recognition of the common law right of self-defense as it relates to international law.[43] Lieutenant Commander Dale Stephens wrote:

> The '*Caroline*' correspondence indicates, however, that the authors themselves drew upon natural law concepts and combined them with municipal notions of self defense as then understood in Anglo-American criminal law. In this regard, the authors were acknowledging the personal and instinctive nature of self defense. Lord Ashburton plainly stated in his response to Mr. Webster of 28 July 1842, that self defense "is the first law of our nature, and it must be recognized by every code which professes to regulate the conditions and relations of man." Further, Lord Ashburton was plainly aware of the novel nature of the American proposition that international actions may be justified by a combination of the established principle of necessity and the national legal concept of self defense. Lord Ashburton specifically noted the 'ingenious' suggestion by Mr. Webster that the legitimacy of British actions should be assessed by reference to this modified concept of self defense under international law. Thus, the British suddenly found themselves defending their Captain's actions on the basis of a principle narrower than self-preservation. Further, Lord Ashburton accepted the challenge and consistently described his justification of British actions in terms analogous to personal self defense.

In 1928, Secretary of State Frank Kellogg, author of the Kellogg-Brian Pact (also known as the Pact of Paris), said: "The right of self defense is inherent in every sovereign state and is implicit in every treaty. Every nation is free at all times and regardless of treaty provisions to defend its territory from attack or invasion and it alone is competent to decide

---

[41]*Id.*

[42]Letter from Daniel Wesbster, Secretary of State, to Lord Ashburton, August 6, 1842, reprinted in 2 John Bassett Moore, A Digest of International Law 409, 412 (1906).

[43]Lieutenant Commander Dale Stephens, *Rules of Engagement and the Concept of Unit Self Defense*, 45 NAVAL L. REV. 126, 134 (1998).

whether circumstances require recourse to war in self defense." The Pact of Paris renounced war as a mechanism to resolve international disputes, and later served as the basis for the charge of crimes against peace prosecuted against the Nazi War Criminals at the Nuremberg International Military Tribunal following World War II. Kellogg recognized that a sovereign nation, by means of its individuals, has an inherent right to defend itself from outside aggressions, and that right was neither created by, nor can be abrogated by, written international law or treaty.

At the International Military Tribunal, Daniel Webster's definition of self-defense was reaffirmed when the Tribunal ruled that the German invasion of Norway in 1940 was not defensive because it was unnecessary to prevent an "imminent" Allied invasion.[44] The Tribunal echoed Webster's criteria for self-defense stating: "preventative action in foreign territory is justified only in case of an instant and overwhelming necessity for self-defense, leaving no choice of means, and no moment of deliberation."[45]

The United Nations was founded to provide a forum in which international disputes could be resolved without resorting to armed force.[46] The United Nation's goal was to substitute a community response for unilateral action in deterring aggression.[47] At the core of the Charter of the United Nations is a prohibition of use of force absent authorization from the Security Council, a body created by the United Nations to oversee international peace.[48] Article 2(4) of the UN Charter provides: "[a]ll Members shall refrain in their international relations from the threat or use of force against the territorial integrity or political independence of any state, or in any other manner inconsistent with the purposes of the United Nations."[49]

---

[44]See International Military Tribunal (Nuremberg), Judgment and Sentences, reprinted in 41 Am J Intl L 172, 205 (1947) ("Preventive action in foreign territory is justified only in case of 'an instant and overwhelming necessity for self-defense, leaving no choice of means, and no moment for deliberation.'"), quoting John Bassett Moore, 2 International Law Digest § 217 at 412 (GPO 1906).

[45]International Military Tribunal, Judgment and Sentences (Oct. 1, 1946), 1 TRIALS MAJ. WAR CRIM 208, 218-22, reprinted in 41 Am J Intl L. 172, 205-207 (1947)

[46]Brunson MacChesney, "Some Comments on the 'Quarantine' of Cuba, *American Journal of International Law*, 57 (No. 3 1963), 593.

[47]Id.

[48]James Francis Gravelle, The Falkland (Malvinas) Islands: An International Law Analysis of the Dispute Between Argentina and Great Britain." *Military Law Review*, 107 (1985), 57.

[49]UN Charter, Article 2(4), _____19__.

The Charter provided two express exceptions to the prohibition on use of force. Article 42 provides that that the Security Council may vote to authorize military force to restore peace.[50] And most importantly, Article 51 recognizes:

> Nothing in the present Charter shall impair the inherent right of individual or collective self defense if an armed attack occurs against a Member of the United Nations until the Security Council has taken the measures necessary to maintain international peace and security. Measures taken by Members in the exercise of the right of self defense shall be immediately reported to the Security Council and shall not in any way affect the authority and responsibility of the Security Council under the present Charter to take at any time such action as it deems necessary in order to maintain or restore international peace and security.[51]

UN Charter Article 51 did not create a new right, it merely codified the pre-existing right all individuals have to self-defense.[52] Article 51 codified the customary international law that existed at time the charter was adopted. At the time, self-defense was defined in terms of the standard set forth in *Caroline* and the application of that standard during the 1946 International Military Tribunal at Nuremberg; necessity and proportionality.

A use of force is necessary if it is in response to a perceived hostile act (armed attack) or perceived demonstration of hostile intent (actions immediately preparatory to an armed attack).[53] Proportionality requires the use of force be reasonable, and not excessive.[54] It must exercise reasonable intensity, duration, magnitude, while *decisively* countering the hostile act or demonstration of hostile intent.[55] A Hostile Act is defined as:

> [a]n attack or other use of force against the United States, U.S. forces, and, in certain circumstances, U.S. nationals, their property, U.S. commercial assets, and/or other designated non-U.S. forces,

---

[50]UN Charter, Article 42, _____.
[51]UN Charter, Article 51, _____.
[52]Byard Q. Clemmons & Gary D. Brown, *Rethinking International Self Defense: The UN's Emerging Role*, NAV. L. REV. 217, 218 (1998). "Self defense is so much a part of state sovereignty that it would be recognized even absent Article 51."
[53]Lieutenant Commander Dale Stephens, *Rules of Engagement and the Concept of Unit Self Defense*, 45 NAVAL L. REV. 126 (1998)
[54]*Caroline*
[55]Id.

foreign nationals and their property. It is also force used directly to preclude or impede the mission and/or duties of U.S. forces, including the recovery of U.S. personnel and vital U.S. Government property.[56]

Demonstrated hostile intent is:

The threat of imminent use of force against the United States, U.S. forces, and in certain circumstances, U.S. nationals, their property, U.S. commercial assets, and/or other designated non-U.S. forces, foreign nationals and their property. Also, the threat of force to preclude or impede the mission and/or duties of U.S. forces, including the recovery of U.S. personnel or vital USG property.[57]

Unfortunately, either due to ignorance or willful risk-aversion, these vigorous and empowering rules of law become severely restricted by the time they trickle down to the individual Soldier.

---

[56]Standing Rules of Engagement, para 5(g).
[57]Standing Rules of Engagement, para 5(h).

CHAPTER 7

CONSTITUTIONAL PROVISIONS

USE OF FORCE IN SELF-DEFENSE AND

THE REASONABLENESS STANDARD

IT IS WELL-SETTLED UNDER THE LAW that individuals have the right to use force to defend against an offensive attack. In Chapter 5, that right was discussed in terms of the "inherent right of self defense;" the natural right of all persons to life, and to defend their life if it is threatened. The inherent right of self-defense provides that a person may use whatever force reasonable and necessary to thwart a threat of death or serious bodily injury. This chapter outlines the provisions of the Constitution governing the use of deadly force by government agents, and argues that these constitutional standards are the same standards applicable to the exercise of military member's inherent right of self-defense, whether here in the United States or when deployed overseas as part of a military operation.

Many so-called "operational law" attorneys in the United States are either ignorant of this huge body of enabling case law or willfully choose to ignore it. These quintessential marplots, either overtly or by their actions, fashion themselves as "internationalists" and, therefore, do not believe that the Constitutional law of the United States has any relevance to their notions of a "superior" International Law. First, such attorneys should remember to what nation they swore allegiance when commissioned as officers. It was not to the U.N., it was to the United States! Secondly,

International Law is nothing more than the composite of time-honored beliefs of nations forged into consensus. Why would we ever shy away from using America's well-founded rules when they make sense and protect our and our allies' forces?

Constitutional Standards

The use of deadly force by law enforcement officers has been the topic of much litigation. Most cases stemming from an officer's use of deadly force allege that the officer used excessive force, which is properly reviewed under the Fourth Amendment's prohibition against unreasonable searches and seizures.[58] The Supreme Court defines "seizure" as a "governmental termination of freedom of movement through means intentionally applied."[59] As there is no greater "termination of freedom of movement" than use of deadly force, law enforcement uses of deadly force are properly considered seizures and subject to the Fourth Amendment reasonableness standard of review.

The constitutionality of use of deadly force is governed by the Fourth Amendment's "objective reasonableness" standard. The Fourth Amendment permits use of deadly force in two general situations: where deadly force is used to protect an officer or others from an immediate threat of death or serious bodily injury; and when deadly force is used to prevent the escape of a fleeing felon where the officer has probable cause to believe the suspect is dangerous, that deadly force is necessary to prevent his or her escape, and some verbal warning is given where it is feasible to do so. In either situation, the officer's actions are judged from the perspective of an objectively reasonable law enforcement officer. As long as any reasonable officer could have reached the same conclusion if faced with the same facts and circumstances, the subject officer's actions are justified under the Fourth Amendment. This is NOT a subjective standard. In other words, we do not determine the reasonableness of an officer's actions simply by polling a number of officers to determine if one officer's actions were reasonable (in

---

[58]U.S. Constitution, Fourth Amendment. Through the incorporation clause of the Fourteenth Amendment, the Fourth Amendment's prohibition of unreasonable searches and seizures has been extended from the federal government to include actions of government at any level (federal, state, local).

[59]Brower v. County of Inyo, 486 U.S. 593 (1989).

their subjective opinions). The standard is "no reasonable officer" could have reached the same conclusion.

To Protect Self or Others

The cornerstone of use of deadly force rule is the right to defend self or others against an immediate threat of death or serious bodily injury. This standard accurately reflects individuals' inherent right of self-defense, and the extension of that right to protect others. If one reasonably believes his life or the life of another is threatened, he may justifiably use deadly force to prevent the attack.

To Prevent Escape

A law enforcement officer may use deadly force to prevent a suspect's escape where it is necessary to prevent said escape, and the officer has probable cause to believe a suspect poses a significant threat of death or serious physical injury to the officer or others.[60] Here, the Supreme Court created a two-pronged test to determine whether or not an officer may use deadly force to prevent a suspect's escape: the officer must have probable cause to believe the suspect poses a significant threat of inflicting serious physical injury on someone, and the use of deadly force must be necessary to prevent escape.

A suspect poses a significant threat of inflicting serious physical injury on a person where by virtue of his physical actions, he has "threaten[ed] the officer with a weapon **or** there [the officer has] probable cause to believe that [the suspect] has committed a crime involving infliction or threatened infliction of serious physical harm."[61] To pose a significant threat, a suspect does not have to present a weapon directed at the officer. That situation would properly be analyzed under the "protect self" category, as the suspect threatened the officer's life by presenting a weapon aimed at the officer. To pose a significant threat justifying use of deadly force to prevent escape, an officer simply must be able to articulate that he had probable cause to believe the suspect committed an offense involving threatened infliction or infliction of serious bodily injury. The officer may or may not readily observe a weapon on the suspect's person, but if he can articulate that the

---

[60]Tennessee v. Garner, 471 US 1 at 4
[61]Id. at 10, emphasis added.

suspect posed a significant threat by virtue of prior actions of threatened or inflicted harm, the officer is justified in using deadly force to affect seizure of that suspect, and prevent his further escape.

For the use of deadly force to be necessary to affect the seizure, the suspect must be unwilling to comply with the officer's attempts to place the suspect in law enforcement custody. Even where a suspect poses a significant threat of inflicting serious bodily injury, if the suspect complies with an officer's commands, or is compliant with an officer's demands, deadly force is not necessary to affect the seizure. However, where a suspect is actively fleeing law enforcement, the suspect is not compliant. In such cases, by virtue of his actions, the suspect poses a significant threat to the bodily integrity of the officer and others, and is non-compliant and unwilling to submit to the law enforcement officer's authority. In such cases, deadly force is necessary to prevent escape, as the officer cannot affect an arrest without subjecting himself to significant risk of being on the receiving end of the suspect's previously demonstrated dangerous tendencies.

In certain circumstances the Supreme Court suggests that an officer should afford a suspect the notice to surrender and be compliant. In such cases, where the situation permits, an officer should attempt to provide a verbal warning to give the suspect an opportunity to comply with the officer's commands. If the suspect complies, use of deadly force is no longer necessary to prevent the suspect's escape. If the suspect fails to comply, deadly force is necessary to prevent escape, and is warranted under the circumstances. A verbal warning is not required in all fleeing suspect cases. Each scenario will dictate whether a warning is feasible given the facts presented the officer. But the main point of the verbal warning is to provide the suspect notice that he is actively being pursued by law enforcement. If a reasonable person would believe the suspect knew that law enforcement was attempting to affect his arrest, and the suspect failed to comply or otherwise submit to the officer's authority, deadly force is authorized.

Therefore, where an officer has probable cause to believe a suspect poses a significant threat of inflicting serious bodily injury and use of deadly force is necessary to prevent his escape, the officer may justifiably use deadly force to prevent the suspect's escape.

Reasonableness Standard

The constitutional standard for use of deadly force by law enforcement was defined by the Supreme Court in the 1985 case *Tennessee v. Garner*.[62] In *Garner*, a law enforcement officer shot and killed an unarmed juvenile burglary suspect (Garner) as he attempted to flee from law enforcement by jumping over a fence. The officer reasoned that if Garner successfully cleared the fence he would evade apprehension. The officer shot Garner pursuant to a Tennessee state statute which authorized law enforcement officers to use "all necessary means," including deadly force to effect the arrest of a fleeing felon. The Supreme Court evaluated the Tennessee statute and the officer's actions under the Fourth Amendment's reasonableness standard. The Court struck down the statute as unconstitutional, holding that "[w]here the suspect poses no immediate threat to the officer and no threat to others, the harm resulting from failing to apprehend him does not justify the use of deadly force to do so."[63] The Court held that use of deadly force is reasonable under the Fourth Amendment where the officer has probable cause to believe the suspect is dangerous, that deadly force is necessary to prevent his escape, and where feasible, a verbal warning is given.[64]

Four years later the Court again considered the Fourth Amendment's reasonableness standard in connection with law enforcement use of force cases. In *Graham v. Connor*, the Court held that a law enforcement officer is justified in using force to effect a seizure where the level of force chosen is "objectively reasonable in light of the facts and circumstances confronting [the officer]¼judged from the perspective of a reasonable officer on the scene, rather than with the 20/20 vision of hindsight."[65] The *Graham* case was not a use of deadly force case, but is instructive in the analysis of what constitutes "objective reasonableness." In *Graham*, Officer Connor observed suspicious activity outside a Charlotte, NC convenience store. He followed the suspicious person to his vehicle, and followed the vehicle approximately one-half of a mile before conducting an investigatory stop. Graham told the officer his sporadic behavior was a result of low blood sugar. The officer detained Graham while he ascertained whether or

[62]471 U.S. 1 (1985).
[63]Garner at 11.
[64]Id. at 11-12.
[65]Graham v. Connor, 490 US 386, 396-97 (1989).

not any criminal activity took place at the convenience store. When Officer
Connor returned to his cruiser to call for back up, Graham exited his car
and ran around it twice before falling and passing out on the curb. Connor,
and several other officers, handcuffed Graham, and used physical control
techniques to affect his arrest. Graham maintained it was his low blood
sugar that caused his behavior. At some later point Officer Connor determined no criminal activity took place at the convenience store and released
Graham without further incident. During the scenario Graham sustained
physical injury, including a broken foot and bumps and bruises. He
brought suit against Officer Connor alleging he used excessive force against
Graham.

The Court held that allegations of excessive force, deadly force or otherwise, are properly analyzed under the Fourth Amendment's objective
reasonableness standard. However, what constitutes a reasonable act is "not
capable of precise definition or mechanical application."[66] What level of
force is reasonable will depend on the facts presented the officer. If another
similarly situated officer would have applied the same level of force had he
known or believed what the officer knew or believed at the time of the incident, then the application of force is considered objectively reasonable. The
law doesn't require the officer to be "right." In fact, there have been several
cases where the court found that when looked at as a Monday-morning
quarterback, the officer's actions weren't reasonable. But when looked at
from the perspective of the officer at the time the use of force was applied,
the actions were reasonable, and therefore constitutional.

When it is all said and done, the Supreme Court has held that law
enforcement officers may use whatever level of force is reasonable in order
to affect an arrest. The decision will be judged from the perspective of the
officer at the time the decision was made, in light of the facts and circumstances known and presented to the officer at the time. For cases involving
deadly force, the reasonableness analysis includes examining whether the
facts and circumstances presented to the officer included a threat of serious
bodily injury to the officer or another person. If so, use of deadly force is
reasonable. If the facts and circumstances presented to the officer indicate
that a fleeing suspect, posed a significant threat to the safety of the officer

[66]Id. at 396.

or another, and the suspect failed to comply with the authority of the officer, deadly force is reasonable and necessary to prevent escape of that dangerous suspect. These are the standards the Supreme Court set forth for law enforcement, as interpreted through the Fourth Amendment of the U.S. Constitution. The standards are highly deferential to the officer, recognizing the officer must make "split second decisions" and doesn't have the luxury of arm-chair tactical analysis. Wherever an officer can articulate and justify his actions based on facts and circumstances he faced, how he handled the situation or what level of force he chose to handle the situation, will likely be deemed reasonable, and constitutional under the Fourth Amendment.

While the Supreme Court has almost exclusively examined the Fourth Amendment's reasonableness requirement in terms of federal, state, and local law enforcement actions, it is not the law enforcement portion of the employee's classification that triggers the Fourth Amendment, but the fact that the officer is carrying out the duties and functions of the government. In fact, in the 2001 case of *Saucier v. Katz*, 533 U.S. 194, the Supreme Court applied this same reasonableness standard of protection to Title 10 Soldiers conducting their duties in CONUS. In Katz, a group of protesters sued the United States alleging that Military Police officers assigned to The Presidio used excessive force when affecting an arrest. Moreover, the Court said that even if the military members were mistaken as to both the facts and the law, their actions were still entitled to qualified immunity so long as their mistakes were reasonable:

"In excessive force cases, in addition to the deference officers receive on the underlying constitutional claim, qualified immunity can apply in the event the mistaken belief was reasonable." *Saucier* at 208.

Despite this clear mandate from the Supreme Court, drafters of rules for the use of force for many CONUS-based operations continue to place unreasonable and tactically unsound restrictions on our Soldiers. Recently, National Guard Soldiers were unnecessarily placed at risk by the insertion of such legally unsupported language as "last resort" "exhaust all lesser means" and "minimum force" into the ROE/RUF for the Southwest Border mission. There, Soldiers would be supporting the U.S. Border Patrol in its attempts to keep out illegal aliens and possible terrorists attempting to enter our County unlawfully.

Law enforcement officers voluntarily place themselves in harms way to protect those who need protecting. They enforce domestic law so that individuals unwilling to abide by the law cannot jeopardize the safety of those that do. Law enforcement officers go through highly specialized training to gain the experience and knowledge necessary to do a physically demanding and dangerous job. In this respect, military personnel engaging in activities related to their role as member of the Armed Forces are not so different. Today, Soldiers voluntarily enroll in the military and voluntarily place themselves in harms way either here or abroad, in order to protect those that need protecting. When deployed, Soldiers enforce international law so that governments, militia, insurgents, or rogue individuals may not carry out unprovoked offensive attacks that threaten the safety and well being of everyday individuals. Soldiers receive specialized training in a multitude of fields to best prepare them to succeed and survive their demanding and dangerous jobs.

Law enforcement officers enjoy the discretion of the "objective reasonableness" test because such discretion is necessary for them to protect themselves *so they can accomplish their missions.*[67] As said in *Maryland v. Soper,*[68] "[s]uch acts of defense are really part of the exercise of [an officer's] official authority. They are necessary to make the enforcement effective."[69] Similarly, U.S. military forces abroad are not only unreasonably put in jeopardy, but are unnecessarily hamstrung in accomplishing their missions if not allowed to adequately defend themselves. For these reasons, American Soldiers should be judged by the same legal requirements for the use of deadly force as law enforcement officers. Their missions may be different, but the end result is the same- enforce the appropriate law, through force if necessary, to protect themselves and others from unjustified, illegal, and unreasonable harm. Soldiers serve the government the same as law enforcement, and face the same tense situations requiring immediate action. Soldiers don't give up their constitutional rights simply by putting on a uniform.

[67]See, e.g., In re Neagle, 135 U.S. 1, 72 (1890); Reed v. Madden, 87 F.2d 846, 852 (8th Cir. 1937); West Virginia v. Laing, 133 F. 887, 891-92 (4th Cir. 1904); Kelly v. Georgia, 68 F. 652 (S.D. Ga. 1895); Ramsey v. Jailer, 20 F. Cas. 214 (D. Ky. 1879); Roberts v. Jailer, 26 F. Cas. 571, 576 (D. Ky. 1867).

[68]270 U.S. 9 (1926) (noting that this case concerned a petition for a writ of mandamus to remand an indictment for the murder of four probation agents).

[69]Id.

The Fourth Amendment "objective reasonableness" standard and *Garner's* application of what is objectively reasonable in using deadly force are identical to Daniel Webster's test for what constitutes a permissible use of deadly force in self-defense. Webster quantified the right in terms of "necessity", and "proportionality." The Constitution quantifies the right in terms of "reasonableness," and the Supreme Court elaborated that reasonableness manifests itself when used to ward off an imminent attack of death or serious bodily injury, or to prevent the escape (and future infliction of harm on another) of a dangerous fleeing felon. According to Webster, a justified use of deadly force in self-defense is one that is necessary to prevent immediate danger of death or serious bodily injury.

If an individual is presented with a threat to his or her life or physical well being, a proportional and reasonable response is to use deadly force to thwart the attack. Offensive (in a legal not tactical understanding) uses of force are unreasonable and unjustified, defensive uses of force are necessary, reasonable, and justified. Webster's necessity and proportionality are identical to the reasonableness requirement of the Fourth Amendment. Necessity means that your life or well being is threatened, and failure to act will result in the expected harm, and proportionality means the response was reasonable given the perceived threat. Necessity justifies the use of deadly force in response to a perceived hostile act or demonstration of hostile intent. Proportionality requires the response to be in kind to the threatened harm. Hostile acts and demonstrations of hostile intent are threats to the life and safety of their intended targets. A reasonable and proportional response is the use of deadly force to stop the threat.

Much of the confusion that emanates from contrasting the Constitutional requirements of reasonableness and Webster's concept of proportionality is the confusion over what "proportional" means legally in the context of the application of deadly force in self-defense. It simply means "a reasonable response to a perceived threat." It does *not* mean a "response in kind" or the dictionary definition of "corresponding in degree and amount." If that were the standard, the law would require officers to bring a knife rather than a firearm to a knife fight. Wisely, neither the law nor common sense requires such inanity. Yet, too often, drafters of modern ROE confuse this point.

The Fourth Amendment and International Law simply require that an act be necessary to stop an imminent threat. The lines between Webster and the Constitution blur, but both recognize the same standard for determining whether a use of deadly force in self-defense is objectively reasonable. As both international law through Article 51 of the UN Charter, and the US Constitution through the Fourth Amendment, recognize the same right and the same standard, it begs to reason that it should be interpreted, taught, and applied in the same manner.

As a last line of defense for our Soldiers, even the Uniform Code of Military Justice, as enunciated in the Dept of Army 27-9, Military Judge's Benchbook, 5-2-1, recognizes the same standards of self-defense as an affirmative defense as there must be "a reasonable belief that death or grievous bodily harm was about to be inflicted." But, despite the bemoaning of the liberal press corps, line of duty shooting decisions should rarely be decided by a criminal court. Unfortunately, within the military system there are no clear administrative mechanisms for formal "shooting review teams" to assess and evaluate the reasonableness of a Soldier's decision. In many cases, commanders send matters all the way to a criminally-focused Article 32 inquiry. Even this, apparently, is not enough for the *Washington Post*.

CHAPTER 8

APPLICATION TO THE MILITARY STANDING RULES OF ENGAGEMENT: THE SROE[70]

IN JUNE 2005, THE PENTAGON QUIETLY CHANGED[71] its Standing Rules of Engagement (SROE). Some classical marplots within the judge advocate community allege this change limits service members' inherent right of individual self-defense. In an unclassified policy dated June 13, 2005, Chairman of the Joint Chiefs of Staff Instruction 3121.01B was modified, allowing commanders, by way of exception, to "limit individual self-defense by members of their unit." The purpose of this change was to clarify a blinding flash of the obvious: a commander can, under certain tactical circumstances, override a subordinate's judgment as to what constitutes an imminent threat. By way of proper example, a commander of a naval vessel may order a missileman to hold fire on a weapons system until a vampire (hostile enemy inbound missile) is within 15 nautical

---

[70]Chairman of the Joint Chiefs of Staff Instruction 3121.01B (13June2005)

[71]During the planning and staffing of this important document, a "switched-on" Senior Department of Defense Attorney was deliberately cut out of the decision-making process. This is unfortunate because this individual—a world-recognized expert in use of force, rules of engagement, and all aspects of operational law—would have brought a voice of reason, as well the experience of two combat tours as a Marine rifleman in Vietnam, to the table. It appears that his opinions concerning ROE and use of force training did not sit well with some of the risk-averse set within the E-Ring of the Pentagon.

miles because the commander knows that the counter-missile system has a much higher kill rate against the vampire if it is allowed to enter a certain window. And the commander's authority can override the individual missileman's notions of what constitutes an imminent threat, even if the individual missileman's notions may, in fact, be reasonable.

Unfortunately, this new SROE provision is being improperly interpreted, as some senior uniformed attorneys—even within the JCS legal office—have already voiced the opinion that "the new change made it clear that individual self-defense no longer existed." Unfortunately, too, some judge advocates have expanded the SROE's exception to mean commanders can and should always limit individual self-defense. Hence, we see such insanity as "use minimum force," "exhaust all lesser means," and "Don't shoot fleeing hostile actors" being written into ROE at the operational and tactical levels.

This is dangerous and imprudent for many reasons. Besides ignoring hundreds of years of legal precedence, if improperly interpreted, it would unnecessarily restrict our service members' ability to defend themselves in a world of increasingly violent, asymmetric threats. If the Army thinks it has a recruiting problem now, wait until the mothers and fathers of prospective recruits learn that the military is trying to give more legal protections to possible Al Qaeda members demonstrating hostile intent than the Fourth Amendment currently gives to criminals in the United States.

For years, a guiding principle in all of America's Rules of Engagement—classified and unclassified—has been the caveat that "nothing in these rules limits the *inherent* right of self-defense." Now, apparently, some within JCS believe that, with the stroke of a regulatory pen, they can some how obviate this inherent right. Their rationale appears to be based on lawyer-contrived scenarios, whereby it is alleged that continuing to recognize a Soldier's inherent right may somehow interfere with some future command authority or specific mission success. No true warrior could ever imagine a situation whereby they, or their subordinates, would stand by and do nothing in the face of an imminent threat designed to inflict death or serious bodily injury on themselves or innocent others. Rather, these rule changes appear to have been written by either entrenched marplots or those more concerned with avoiding potentially embarrassing political fallout if one of our Soldiers mistakenly shoots the pizza deliveryman rather than a true bad actor. This tension has existed in law enforcement for decades, but proper training—*not* more restrictive rules—is the answer.

Those in military uniform—just as police officers do—sign up to voluntarily put themselves into harm's way. They do not, however, sign up to get attacked without having the authority and ability to defend themselves *at will* when faced with an imminent threat.

It is also highly questionable as to how such a regulation could be lawfully implemented. Any order attempting to restrict self-defense would contradict our Code of Conduct, which states that American fighting forces should not surrender when they have the means to resist.

Of greater legal consequence, however, is that every American's inherent right of self-defense predates the Constitution itself. "The right of self-defense…is found in the law of nature, and it is not, nor can be superseded by any law of society." *Sir Michael Foster, Crown Cases* (1762).

"There does exist therefore, gentlemen, a law which is a law not of the statute-book, but of nature; a law which we possess not by instruction, tradition, or reading, but which we have caught, imbided, and sucked in at Nature's own breast; a law which comes to us not by education but by constitution, not by training but by intuition—the law, I mean, that should our life have fallen into any snare, into the violence and the weapons of robbers or foes, every method of winning a way to safety would be morally justifiable." Markus Tullius Cicero (circa 60 B.C.), *Cicero: On Behalf of Milo.*

Those in uniform—those most likely to exercise such a right—do not surrender this inherent right upon enlistment into the armed forces.

What Do the Rules of Engagement Currently Provide?

Changing ROE in a manner that diminishes our warriors' ability to defend themselves sends a bad message from on high. Moreover, it reduces their tactical preparedness and ability to respond to an imminent threat. Much has been made recently concerning deficiencies of armored Humvees and other tactical equipment necessary to work more safely in Iraq. If, however, service members do not possess the fundamental ability to act quickly and appropriately against a perceived threat and, as importantly, a clear understanding of their legal authority to do so, the latest equipment will do little to save their lives. Not every target that presents itself is hostile and not every situation requires deadly force. But, if so confronted, Soldiers need to know that their command will stand behind them if they have to make such a decision under tense, uncertain, and rapidly evolving situations. This change to the SROE—the bedrock of all classified and unclassified rules of engagement—and an overly-restrictive interpretation thereof will cause further hesitation amongst the troops and very possibly, more unnecessary deaths.

Despite the confusion created both by the new SROE and its misinterpretation by some overzealous marplots, it still contains the following powerful directive to all commanders (not judge advocates!):

Unit Commanders at all levels shall ensure that individuals within their respective units understand and are trained on when and how to use force in self-defense. Para. 1.b.

Sadly, commanders are not aware of this directive, ignore it, or abdicate their responsibilities under it to judge advocates that are not interested or skilled enough to properly train and advise their clients.

Lastly, among judge advocates and commanders, there is great confusion over what "use proportionate force" means. Much of the confusion flows from inappropriately and unnecessarily trying to wedge the concept of "proportionate force" that appears in the Law of Armed Conflict (or the Law of War) into the ROE/RUF matrix. The Law of Armed Conflict concept requiring nations to use only proportionate force during periods of hostilities is designed to prevent nations from responding to a minor border incursion with all out war (or targeting a squad-sized element hiding in an urban area with a 2,000 lb bomb). The concept of proportionality in international law has everything to do with limiting collateral damage and preventing the escalation of hostilities and nothing to do with limiting the amount of force an individual uses to defend himself. More frighteningly, confused judge advocates add insult to this injury by morphing the word "proportional" into "minimum." The result is that troops are regularly briefed that they are to defend themselves-not with *proportionate* force, not to eliminate the threat, but with *minimum* force.

This language is briefed perhaps due to commanders' or judge advocates' underestimation of troops' capacity to appreciate proportionality. In other words, troops are briefed to use "minimum force" in self-defense as a shorthand measure in an effort to preclude "excessive force." However, as Colonel (Ret.) W. Hays Parks has quite accurately, proclaimed: "Minimum deadly force is an oxymoron."[72]

The trigger for the use of deadly force should be necessity. The legal criterion by which the service member's decision to open fire will be evaluated should be that of "objective reasonableness" as explained by *Graham v. Connor*.

In a full up, force on force war with declared hostiles, there is no concern for when a serviceman fires, how long or how often he fires, so long as it is directed at the enemy. But in today's world, the "enemy" is not such a clear-cut target. Instead, our troops are deployed on counter-terrorist, peacekeeping, humanitarian aid, and security assistance missions. And no enemy is currently wearing fashionable "AQ" (Al Qaeda) T-Shirts by which they can instantly be identified.

---

[72]Parks, supra note 3, at 36.

CHAPTER 9

LIABILITY AND POLICY

Liability: n. The quality or state of being legally obligated or accountable; legal responsibility to another or to society, enforceable by civil remedy or criminal punishment. (Black's Law Dictionary, 7th ed.)

Legal Liability

LIABILITY IS PERHAPS ONE OF THE MOST OVERUSED and incorrectly applied words in the average bureaucrat's vocabulary. As stated above, liability is properly defined as a legal obligation to another, enforceable by civil remedy or criminal penalty. The definition of liability does <u>not</u> include *exposure* to lawsuits, *exposure* to criticism, or *exposure* to civil rights group or media scrutiny. Bureaucrats and managers, however, throw the excuse of "liability" anytime they don't want to back their Soldiers or officers either post-shooting or "pre-shooting" (by providing solid, aggressive training) because they fear lawsuits, criticism, and bad press. In the past, this has created a CYA environment more focused on preventing criticism than carrying out a mission or protecting innocents from harm. In the view of many police officers, it is suspected that their politically-appointed superiors would rather conduct a state funeral for a slain officer than deal with the political fall-out from a police shooting. Indeed, many ignorant yet politically-motivated prosecutors have criminally charged police officers to placate a vocal and ignorant minority.[74]

Unfortunately, this same mind-set has crept into many risk-averse military commanders' parlance. The root of the "liability excuse" is the lawyers. Lawyers toss out "liability" as a reason not to do something either when there is legitimate concern that the proposed action will result in actual legal culpability and obligation (which is good) or when as a policy matter they don't want to authorize a specific task, and it is easier to say "no" (which is bad).

For some attorneys, it is too difficult to take the time and understand the dynamics of the issue raised, or admit that it is not a legal question, but a policy question outside the realm of the lawyer's expertise. Poor operational law attorneys will never admit that they don't know something and when in doubt, will come up with an excuse like liability. The reality is that the United States Government is liable for wrongful or negligent acts of its employees in very limited circumstances. In most cases, the Federal Tort Claims Act is the exclusive remedy for an individual to seek redress from the Government for injury sustained at the hands of a federal employee.[75] However, the Federal Tort Claims Act explicitly excludes from coverage any claim arising out of the combatant activities of the armed forces during times of war[76], injury that occurred in a foreign country[77], or injury to military personnel arising from activity incident to service[78]. In addition, the Foreign Claims Act[79] recognizes liability only for certain acts and omissions by armed forces personnel arising in foreign countries that relate to noncombatant activities. Alleged injury or harm arising from a combat activity is expressly excluded from coverage or liability.

The United States cannot be held liable for any alleged harm resulting from a combat-related activity arising in a foreign country, such as discharge of a firearm in self-defense. There are no documented cases where the United States was sued civilly for a death resulting from a soldier exercising

[74]E.g., Atlanta Police Officer Ray Bunn was criminally indicted in December 2005 for an in-line-of-duty shooting that occurred in July 2002, when he properly and lawfully shot a car theft suspect who attempted to run him and his partner over with a Chevrolet SUV.
[75]28 U.S.C. §2671 et seq.
[76]28 U.S.C. §2680(j).
[77]28 U.S.C. §2680(k).
[78]Feres v. United States, 340 U.S. 135, 146 (1950).
[79]28 U.S.C. §2734 et seq.

his right to self-defense during combat. There is no legal procedure for such a lawsuit, and no such suit has been entertained. The fear that the Government may be liable for a death caused by a soldier exercising self-defense is unsupported and absurd.

An individual soldier may be held criminally liable for wrongful actions in accordance with the Uniform Code of Military Justice. In a situation where a soldier causes the death of another person, he may be charged with either murder[80] or manslaughter[81]. To successfully prosecute a soldier for murder, the court must find that the individual killed another without justification or excuse when he had premeditated the killing, intended to kill or inflict great bodily harm, was engaged in an inherently dangerous act that showed a wanton disregard for human life, or at the time of the death was engaged in or attempted to engaged in burglary, sodomy, rape, robbery, or aggravated arson[82].

To successfully prosecute a soldier for manslaughter, the court must find that the accused intended to kill or inflict great bodily harm, and did so in the heat of the moment after adequate provocation, or without intent to kill or inflict great bodily harm, kills another as a result of his negligence, or while committing another criminal act other than burglary, sodomy, rape, robbery, or aggravated arson[83]. Self-defense serves as an excuse to murder or manslaughter when the accused *reasonably* believed that death or great bodily harm was imminent and that the taking of life was necessary to protect him from death or serious bodily harm.[84]

Likewise, armed forces personnel cannot be held individually civilly liable for injury or harm suffered by another during his exercise of combat-related activities.[85] Neither the United States Government nor individual soldier can be held civilly liable for a third party death occurring during combat-related activities in a foreign country. In addition, self-defense is available as a complete excuse to any criminal charge arising from the death

[80]UCMJ Art 118, 10 U.S.C. §918.
[81]UCMJ Art 119, 10 U.S.C. §919.
[82]UCMJ Art 118, 10 U.S.C. §918.
[83]USMJ Art. 119, 10 U.S.C. §919.
[84]United States v. Jackson, 15 USCMA 603 (1966); United States v. Snyder, 6 USCMA 692 (1956); United States v. Gordon, 14 USCMA 314 (1963); United States v. Dearing, 60 MJ 892 (1005, NMCCA).
[85]Chappell v. Wallace, 462 U.S. 296 (1983); United States v. Stanley, 483 U.S. 669, 674 n.2, 680-81 (1987).

where the accused reasonably believed they faced a risk of death or serious bodily injury and self-defense was necessary to prevent the harm. No legal liability extends from the Government to any person in these cases.

Criticism Is Not Liability

While no legal liability extends from a soldier's reasonable exercise of self-defense there may be circumstances where the soldier, his unit, or branch of service may be publicly or politically criticized depending on the circumstances of the death. Criticism is not the same as legal liability. One imposes a legal obligation for remedy; the other is merely perception and disapproval. Lawyers and commanding officers need to be careful not to confuse the two and prohibit a certain action arguing "liability," when really what motivates the prohibition is fear of criticism. While it is easy to judge a soldier's actions from the perspective of an easy chair in Peoria, Illinois, that is not the legal standard for reasonable application of force in self-defense. Any criticism stemming from the lazy-boy observer should never affect operations overseas, no matter how public or loud the criticism. To put it another way, as a Marine Lieutenant Colonel at Quantico recently stated: "If someone orders my Marines to abandon or limit their right of self-defense, I have a duty to disregard that order."

The same is true in response to media representations of operations overseas. On November 13, 2004, a U.S. Marine was captured on video shooting an apparently unarmed wounded Iraqi in the head as he entered an unsecured Mosque that the Marines engaged kinetically just moments before. The troops were attacked by insurgents hiding in the Mosque. This was the identical insurgent group that attacked the same Marines the day before, while they were providing medical assistance to civilians and even wounded insurgents. Kevin Sites, the reporter imbedded with the Marines, videotaped the Marine entrance into the Mosque, observed multiple Iraqi casualties in the room, and, when one of the insurgents moved his arm upwards, the Marine raised his rifle and shot the Iraqi twice in the head. This action, later inflammatorily referred to by the media as the "double tap in Fallujah" followed mission intelligence that revealed Iraqi fighters were taking amphetamines and adrenaline to boost performance, and were booby-trapping their dead and wounded to inflict casualties on U.S. troops when searched or given medical care. The day before the incident, the Marine in question lost a teammate to a similar booby-trapped Iraqi body. Just hours before the incident at the Mosque, a booby-trapped Iraqi body killed one Marine and injured five others. Given this intelligence, a Marine unit commander authorized Soldiers to shoot any male on the street between 15 and 50 who posed a security risk, regardless of whether they possessed a weapon.

Marines were authorized to use their best judgment in threat assessment and elimination. The Marine entered a building containing known enemy combatants. It was known practice for the insurgents to pretend to be dead or wounded and use their suicide martyrdom to further their cause and kill U.S. troops. When the one individual raised his arm the Marine made a split second decision to eliminate that threat. After the incident, Mr. Sites released the video, including identities of the Marines to the media pool in Iraq. The entire video was broadcast and immediately faced criticism from the arm chair observers back in the comfort of the United States. The media recklessly accused the Marine of violating the Geneva Convention, which prohibits killing a warrior who is *hors de combat*. The media scrutinized the Marine Corps for its rules of engagement permitting the elimination of adult males regardless of whether they possessed a weapon, arguing that lax rules of engagement permitted Marines to make decisions based on the situation they face rather than restrictive rules of engagement created and taught prior to engagement with the enemy. The Marine involved in the incident was removed from his unit pending criminal investigation by the Marine Corps. In May of 2005, an Article 32 investigation (similar to a civilian grand jury) report exonerated the Marine, finding that he acted in self-defense when he shot the wounded Iraqi. The report held that because insurgents in the area made a practice of bobby-trapping their dead and wounded, the soldier was justified in firing his weapon to eliminate a reasonably perceived threat.

While ultimately the Marine was cleared of any wrongdoing, the investigation took the better part of six months to complete. During that time he was not permitted to return to his unit. The media took a portion of a video shot during a week long siege, and publicly criticized the Marine, the Marine Corps, and the military leaders who authorized the Marines to make decisions based on the situation they faced. As a result, the military took heat from the media and from powerful politicians, and has since attempted to restrict the authority of troops overseas to shoot adult males posing a security risk.

The political and risk-averse set constantly clamor for more restrictive rules of engagement, arguing that by shooting suspected insurgents that might pose a threat of death or serious bodily injury, the US is "alienating" more and more Iraqis and creating more insurgents. The unspoken statement by such cowards[86] is that Soldiers, Sailors, Airmen and Marines are supposed to stand fast and "take one on the chin" for the greater good. This is pure balderdash. First, it is legally and morally indefensible. Second, it shows an unnecessary weakness to our enemies and sends the clear message that America does not have the will to defend herself.

Policy Considerations

The law often appears as a complicated, convoluted mess of backwards thinking, written by lawyers who believe it makes them appear smart if they use big words and run-on sentences. In the same manner, the law is much akin to a computer operating system like MS-DOS. Except for the few nerds who go to special school to learn how to interpret and apply MS-DOS, most lay people have no clue what MS-DOS actually is. Those same nerds that now have been to school and know what MS-DOS is, create an interface between MS-DOS and the user. It's supposed to be user friendly, but often it is just as confusing and frustrating as MS-DOS itself; that is, if any of us knew or could even recognize MS-DOS if it hit us over the head. Often, what one really needs is help from someone who is not specifically trained in MS-DOS, but understands the operating system and how it works on a practical level and who can then translate the operating system into English by way of a "how to guidebook." That book takes all the fluff out and gives you exactly what you need to know in order to operate the computer. Sure, you end up operating MS-DOS, but you're doing it through application, not by directly thinking in terms of MS-DOS. When you're up against a deadline and can't find the document you worked on for umpteen hours, it doesn't matter what the command prompt for "search all

---

[86]Note, that those proposing such idiocies are never the end-users of the restrictive rules.

files and folders" is. It only matters that you can go to the Start menu, search for the file and print it in time to make your deadline.

The law is like MS-DOS. It's a confusing garble of precedent, statutes, and judicial musings all coming together and creating the binding principles under which we are required to operate. Lawyers go to the special school to learn how to think like a lawyer and decipher the garbled mess. Because Soldiers and cops do not need to know what case from 1986 it was where the Supreme Court found it reasonable to use deadly force in effecting an arrest, but do need to know the parameters for when they can apply the principle, lawyers and non-lawyers create policy. Policy is designed to give agency or department-specific positions on specific legal theories. They are designed like the operating system mentioned above, creating an interface between the legal mumbo-jumbo and the user. However, policy is not designed to be a teaching tool, but rather a quick reference guide for big picture themes. That's where the "how to" teaching guide comes in. Soldiers must be given training in advance of encountering situations where they will be forced to make specific decisions about what course of action is appropriate and reasonable. They need the "how to" book for engaging with the enemy, and what constitutes self-defense, which is judgment-based reality training.

When faced with a growing number of "questionable" shootings, Military units must avoid the reactive posture of "ratcheting down on the ROE." Rather, a move towards judgment based training is what is needed. When the concepts of law and policy are taught in training, Soldiers are better equipped to handle situations they face in combat. What is unacceptable, yet is happening with greater frequency, is the growing fear that any use or application of force during war will be unfairly or unnecessarily scrutinized. Such scrutiny, especially without proper judgment-based training, can create deadly hesitation among Soldiers.

Soldiers hear about the Marine in Fallujah and the lengthy investigation taking six months, so when they are faced with a similar situation, they are more likely to gamble with their lives just a few moments longer. "I'll wait until I see whether he's armed or not." Or, "I should go physically confirm their condition." These hesitations routinely get cops killed. Soldiers need to be taught the guidebook to self-defense: threat assessment and elimination. Soldiers need to have a supporting command staff that recognizes the dynamics of the situations these Soldiers face in Indian country. Absent such command support, Soldiers at least need to recognize and understand that making the split-second decision to act may earn them a CID investigation and possibly even a court-martial, but they will be alive to do it. Like the Marine in Fallujah, reasonable uses of force will be cleared on investigation, and risking your life or the lives of other troops is not worth the hesitation.

There's a saying in the legal defense world that it's better to be judged by twelve than carried by six. You may face an investigation following a use of deadly force in self-defense, and in rare cases, a criminal prosecution. But you'll be alive to face them, and ultimately, the law supports reasonable uses of deadly force. Despite media criticism, supervisor scrutiny, and anything else they can throw at you, self-defense is authorized when you reasonably perceive your life is threatened with death or serious bodily injury. Nothing else matters.

CHAPTER 10

MISUNDERSTANDING THE TACTICAL DYNAMICS OF AN ENCOUNTER

The race is not to the swift or the battle to the strong...but time and chance happen to them all.

—Ecclesiastes 9:11

MUCH OF THE DANGER FOUND RECENTLY in some ROE guidance from Southwest Asia—"use minimum force," "don't shoot fleeing hostile actors," "last resort" language, and "escalation of force" cards—emanates not only from the drafters' ignoring the relevant bodies of the law discussed in the last chapter, but also from their woeful ignorance of the tactical dynamics of a deadly force encounter.

There are many ways to break down the tactical dynamics of a deadly force encounter, but the opinions and concepts of most experts can be dovetailed into the following three categories: Action versus Reaction; Tache-Psyche Effect; and, Wound Ballistics. Not only does the relevant case law recognize these factors when assessing the efficacy or lawfulness of a shooting, but commanders, judge advocates and tactical instructors must be intimately familiar with them before attempting to write and teach in this arena. Unfortunately, there are too many so-called "firearms experts"— to include combat arms officers and judge advocates—who have never grasped the fundamentals of these dynamics.

Action Versus Reaction

Bad guys—be they insurgents in Iraq or criminals on the streets of New Orleans—only have one decision: when to initiate an attack. This is true whether it is when to press the "clacker" on an improvised explosive devise, when to fire the first shot in an ambush, or when to fire on a police officer conducting a "routine" car stop. Good guys (and we are always the "good guys")—unless involved in a preplanned offensive or direct action mission—have at least three decision points to assess before initiating action:

First Decision Point. One has to first recognize the threat. Far too often, due to a combination of poor threat recognition training, bad luck, poor situational awareness, and perhaps a skilled opponent, the good guys get "shot in the face" before even recognizing a threat exists. "Good guys can never afford to be unlucky, and bad guys need only be lucky once" is one of the constant messages tactical operators need to remember. John C. Hall, perhaps the preeminent expert on the laws concerning Use of Force, is fond of reminding students that we must not forget the role chance plays in every encounter. He routinely cites to Ecclesiastes 9:11 when lecturing to emphasize the role that chance always plays in encounters.

Second Decision Point. After recognizing a threat, goods guys have to determine an appropriate level of response, because not all threats require a deadly force response. This is why it is extremely important not to burden them with a checklist of conditions that must be met before deadly force is authorized. "Last resort" language in particular is foolhardy because deadly force may, in fact, be the first resort in such an encounter. Another factor that negatively impacts on this second decision point is a factor known as "Hick's Law." A psychologist[87] wrote a 123-page article describing what is a blinding flash of the obvious: the more factors a brain has to filter, the longer it takes to reach a decision. Unfortunately, too many judge advocates

---

[87] W. E. Hick. On the rate of gain of information. Quarterly Journal of Experimental Psychology, 4:11-26, 1952. R. Hyman. Stimulus information as a determinant of reaction time. Journal of Experimental Psychology, 45:188-196, 1953. Hick's law, or the Hick-Hyman law, is a human-computer interaction model that describes the time it takes for a user to make a decision as a function of the possible choices he or she has. Given n equally probable choices, the average reaction time T required to choose among them is approximately $T = b\log_2(n + 1)$ where b is a constant that can be determined empirically by fitting a line to measured data. See also, Stuart K. Card, Thomas P. Moran, Allen Newell (1983). The Psychology of Human-Computer Interaction. According to Card, Moran, and Newell (1983), the +1 is "because there is uncertainty about whether to respond or not, as well as about which response to make."

in charge of drafting ROE ignore this fact. Confusing and tactically impractical advice presented on ROE and EOF cards, like the ones represented below (from domestic relief operations in the wake of Hurricane Katrina and combat operations in Iraq), build in delays and create hesitancy among shooters:

Soldier Rules for Use of Force
Katrina Relief Operation

You have been issued a weapon with ammunition. The intent of these rules is to ensure the maximum level of safety for the Soldier and for the public.

1. Insert an empty magazine into the weapon during routine operations. A battle buddy must confirm that it is an empty magazine before inserting. Magazines with rounds will be carried in ammo pouches on LCV/LBE.

2. Do not insert a magazine with rounds unless ordered. Do not chamber a round until ordered.

3. Do not use deadly physical force to protect property. Firing a weapon is a use of deadly physical force.

4. You may use physical force to defend yourself or others from the use of physical force by an assailant. Do not use more physical force than necessary to repel or fend off the assailant. Physical force does not include the use of deadly physical force.

5. You may not use deadly physical force unless there is imminent danger of serious bodily injury or death to you or others. Use of deadly physical force is a last resort.

6. You may not use deadly physical force if injury can be avoided by retreating. You have a duty to try to withdraw (State Code: retreat) from an assailant if possible to avoid using deadly physical force.

7. Do not initiate any threat of force of any kind that is unnecessary.

8. If any type of force is used, it must be **equal** to the threat you believe is presented. If no deadly threat is presented, you may **not** use deadly force.

9. These Rules may be changed if ordered to another neighboring state.

Approved for Hurricane Katrina operations, 28 August 2005, OSJA, JFHQ-AL

Escalation of Force (EOF) "Smart Card" Issued to Soldiers in Iraq— Fall of 2005

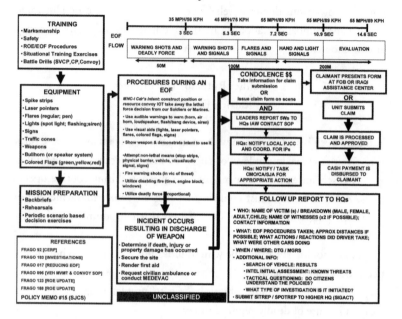

Third Decision Point. Assuming one recognizes the threat and then determines that deadly force is an appropriate level of response, our brain housing group then has to tell our bodies to react. This step, all by itself, can take an average of 1.5 seconds under ideal circumstances. By way of reference, a law enforcement study presented experienced cops with a range scenario whereby the first two decision points were already solved: the threat is a steel target at fifteen meters distance and the appropriate level of response is deadly force. On command (the sounding of an air horn), the officers were to draw and fire on the steel targets. The average response time was over 1.5 seconds: an eternity in a fire fight.

For this reason alone, we must divorce ourselves from the old "Gunsmoke" theory of a gunfight. That 1950s and 1960s era television series' opening credits often showed its protagonist, Marshal Matt Dillon, waiting until the "bad guy" drew first before Matt would draw and shoot. This is Hollywood at its finest, but deadly if used as a model for any use of force situation.

The police officers firing in the controlled study, above, were firing in a controlled setting, at static targets, and were expecting it. Real world decision-making is further negatively impacted because shooting incidents are most often characterized by:

- Sudden, unexpected occurrences (This is nearly always true, because if an incident is expected, presumably one would bring something larger than a handgun or rifle!)

- Rapid and unpredictable movement by target(s) and, hopefully, the shooter.

- Limited target opportunities.

- Frequently under low light or from partially obstructed vantage points

- Life and death stress of sudden, close, personal violence, which leads us to the second dynamic of a tactical encounter, the Tache-Psyche Effect.

Tache-Psyche Effect
We are fearfully and wonderfully made.
- Psalm 139:14

This is how your body may react when you are engaged in mortal combat due to two autonomic functions that occur when one recognizes a life threatening situation. This effect is induced via a psychological function. In other words, one must perceive the threat as serious. Hence, this effect can be heavily attenuated by training. Nevertheless, once perceived, the following physiological effects may follow:

1. Norepinephrine and epinephrine is dumped into the bloodstream.

2. Both heart rate and contractility of the heart increases, leading to increased blood flow.

3. Vasoconstriction—the body's involuntarily action of drawing blood from one's extremities to the central cortex in order to provide maximum oxygenation of vital organs and brain housing group—occurs to the major organs of the body, excluding the brain, and vasodilation occurs to the major muscle groups. The need for digestion is minimal, but you need as much strength in your arms and legs as possible. The brain is never shorted on blood supply, even in the cold, although it is reduced after eating.

4. Body temperature increases, blood pressure increases, and pupils dilate. This may result in a small loss of close focus.

5. Perspiration increases.

6. Blood sugar increases, allowing more energy transfer to the major muscles.

Most are familiar with examples of enhanced strength and heart rate increases associated with the adrenaline dump, but many are unfamiliar with the effects of vasoconstriction and the other physiological and psychological effects of adrenaline.

In 2004, author and retired Army Ranger Dave Grossman published his book *On Combat*, detailing these effects on warriors and police officers under high stress situations. Grossman's book, as well as John Hall's and Urey Patrick's *In Defense of Self and Others*, should be required reading for any commander, judge advocate or staff officer involved in the drafting and training of rules concerning the use of force. Lieutenant Colonel Grossman and others have identified certain physiological and psychological phenomena that occur under situations of close personal violence, to include:

Loss of fine motor skills. This "clubbiness" of fingers further degrades one's ability to draw, reload and manipulate weapon systems. This phenomenon is another reason why guidance such as "don't load a round into the chamber unless confronted with an imminent threat" is sheer folly. Such guidance, however, has become ubiquitous both in combat zones as well as domestic relief operations such as those in response to Hurricane Katrina.

Cognitive processing deteriorates. The warrior's fight or flight response is at its highest level. Many police officers die screaming for help into their radio microphones or repeatedly ordering armed subjects to "drop the weapon" when, instead, they should be engaging the bad guy with overwhelming deadly force.

Auditory Exclusion. Many police officers and Soldiers never hear their own weapons discharge during a fire fight. Sir Winston Churchill noted this phenomenon in one of his many memoirs. Recalling his participation in the last horse cavalry charge of the British Empire at the Battle of Omdurman in the Sudan (September 2 , 1898), Churchill wrote that despite the rattle of musketry, the crash of artillery, the thundering of horse hoof beats, and all the sounds attendant to a modern battlefield, it was "like watching a silent movie." Officers and Soldiers need to understand that they may not hear their partners' warnings or threat activities or vocalizations. This can be very disconcerting if they are not prepared for it.

Time-Space Distortion. Anyone who has been in an automobile accident and saw the accident unfolding before impact—such as when losing control on a long patch of black ice or when looking into the rear view mirror and seeing the idiot behind standing on his brakes as his car screeched toward impact with your vehicle—has probably experienced time-space distortion. What takes mere seconds may appear to take minutes as our brain goes into the "Oh Shit!" mode. This often happens to combatants, who have variously reported seeing their empty brass cartridges discharging in slow motion (sometimes appearing "as large as trash cans") or actually see their bullets impact into their target. Experienced warriors and athletes can sometimes tune their bodies to use this phenomenon to their advantage, such as Ted Williams' claimed ability to slow a 93 mph fastball down to the point where he could see the seams on the ball. Not many folks realize that Ted Williams was also an ace Marine fighter pilot in WW II and Korea. His uncanny ability to control time-space distortion, as well as his superior hand-eye coordination, most likely made him a great fighter pilot, too. Again, if not prepared for this, it can be very disconcerting and further negatively impact on shooters' decisions to use force in a timely and appropriate manner.

According to a former Command Psychologist for one of the military's special mission units, this can effect can be both attenuated and trained-up. This is the concept of being, "in the zone" to which professional athletes train. Special mission operators often report the ability to work as if the world were in slow motion.

Loss of peripheral vision (tunnel vision). FBI records of police officer involved shootings often reflect that officers initially shoot at the suspect's hands. This is not a case of officers trying to "shoot the weapons out of the suspects' hands"—another inane Hollywood concept that is tactically impracticable—but rather a case of the officers being afflicted with tunnel vision. In other words, they initially perceive the weapon rather than the shooter as the threat. Since hands follow the eyes, they begin shooting at the weapon rather than the true danger: the human operating the weapon. Sadly, because they are shot and incapacitated or killed, many never get the opportunity to shift fire to the perpetrator. Experienced operators—SWAT teams and members of Special Mission Units—train to shake themselves out of tunnel vision by constantly scanning their environments as they move through an objective.

Loss of bowel and bladder control. Again, since our autonomic systems switch into gear during violent, life or death struggles, one of the bodily functions that is not important to surviving the moment is retention of waste fluid and fecal matter. Experienced operators recognize this fact, hence their conscious decision before raids and missions to take a "battle crap" to void their bodies prior to their brain housing groups doing this for them during the fight.

Memory Gaps. Often, persons involved in high-stress events forget much of what themselves and others did during the event. Sometimes, after a period of at least 24 hours of decompression, their memory is restored somewhat. That is why it is critical that commanders do not allow criminal investigators (Army CID or local homicide investigators) to interview participants in a line of duty shooting until after this period has lapsed. Moreover, the fact that the recollections of the shooter, other participants, and the physical evidence—for example the number of rounds fired and their direction—might be wildly divergent should not suggest or imply untruthfulness on anyone's behalf.

Intrusive Thoughts. A participant's mind, under the high-stress of a gun fight, may think of things entirely unrelated to the critical events at hand.

Every one of these effects, and every pre-conceived and ill-conceived bad notion we drag to a fire fight interferes with our ability to process information in a timely manner. The good news is that effective, hard training can do much to attenuate these ill effects. It is judgment-based training, however, that is important, not silly rules.

Wound Ballistics

Again, Hollywood has done much to distort and craft our perceptions and beliefs concerning how bullets work and their effect on the human body. Years of portraying suspects getting blown through plate glass windows by Clint Eastwood's .44 Magnum or vehicles exploding or rolling over after being hit by small arm's fire, has created deeply imbedded myths that must be exposed. For it is these myths that are partially to blame for the stupidity found in many examples of ROE guidance and training. These myths, too, are believed not only by unknowing legal advisors, but also by a large number of so-called "combat arms" officers.

When traveling throughout the CENTCOM area of responsibility, many Soldiers in the unit to which the author was assigned were armed with a .45 caliber M1911 handgun (as opposed to the more ubiquitous 9mm Beretta used by most line troops and officers). Many times, he and fellow members in this command were approached by Soldiers, who would exclaim" "I bet that has lots of knock-down power!" or "I heard if you hit someone in the shoulder with a .45 round, it will spin them around!"[88]

The truth is that many police officers, Soldiers—as well as the bad guys—do not even know that they are shot until after the gunfight is over. Unless a person receives a devastating head shot or the cervical spine is severed—causing immediate disruption of the brain housing group and brain nerve function—the body, physically, can keep on fighting until volumic blood loss (around 40%) deprives the brain-nerve function of enough oxygen to function. That is why guidance should never be "use minimum force" or "shoot and assess," but rather "you should apply force until the threat is over." That is the standard to which Soldiers, Sailors, Airmen and Marines should train to, not "use minimum force."

But before one can understand why this is so, gaining an understanding of how bullets work is critically important. Bullets work both psychologically and physically.

How Bullets Work Psychologically
Many have preconditioned their minds into believing how bullets work. Again, Hollywood is responsible for most of this folly. The FBI, in its

[88]As further evidence of the woeful ignorance of firearms possessed by many "combat arms" officers and noncommissioned officers, the unit commander was also routinely advised—with a huge hint of caution—"Sir, did you know that your pistol is cocked!" The standard, combat-ready carry mode of any Model 1911 .45 pistol is "cocked and locked" or "Condition One." To the uninitiated—especially those reared in the risk-averse environment of the military, where Soldiers are routinely instructed "do not even load a round in the chamber unless confronted with an imminent threat," the presence of a cocked and locked pistol was doubly frightening! The Commander would often simply respond with, "Yes, I know," and then walk away from the dumbfounded individual. More often than not, though, he would give a succinct education on the five safety mechanisms present on a Condition One M1911: grip safety, manual thumb safety, internal firing pin disconnect, trigger finger and muzzle discipline.

exhaustive studies of law enforcement related shootings, has found many examples of experienced police officers winning the initial phase of a gunfight by accurately engaging suspects, then ultimately losing by not finishing the mission. Some of these instances have been caused by cops, in the middle of a firefight, stopping and actually looking at their own weapons because they weren't "working like they were supposed to work." In other words, the cops had preconditioned their expectations as to how a suspect who they had just shot was supposed to react. And when the suspects did not immediately fall to the ground (or get blown backwards or through the plate glass window), it caused a moment of hesitation on the cop's part, sometimes with fatal consequences.

More importantly, instead of immediately falling to the ground, suspects sometime continued to aggressively assault or return fire on the officers. In the first 10 seconds of the famous and tragic FBI shootout of April 1986 in Miami, Florida, FBI Special Agent Jerry Dove fired a Winchester Silver Tip 9mm hollow nosed round into one of the suspects, Michael Platt. This round severed Platt's right brachial artery before it entered his upper thoracic cavity where it collapsed his right lung and caused further arterial bleeding. That one round fired by Jerry Dove caused a fatal injury to Platt. That means, by expert medical opinion provided post-incident, it was believed that even had Platt received immediate trauma care, he still would have expired.

But, Michael Platt didn't perish for an additional four minutes until he either exsanguinated (bled out) or succumbed to a head shot administered by FBI Agent Ed Mireles during the closing moments of the firefight. But, in this additional four minutes, Platt killed two FBI Agents, including Jerry Dove, and grievously wounded five others. While the mechanics or physical aspects of wound ballistics—how and why it took so long for the suspects to "bleed out"—played a role in their ability to continue the fight, it was the suspects' psychological determination that proved so deadly to the FBI. Yet, despite the damage received by the FBI, they also managed some "pay back" of their own that very day:

"All five of the FBI Agents who were wounded continued to function and fight back despite their wounds. The best example for this discussion is FBI Special Agent Ed Mireles. SA Mireles had lost the use of his left arm due to a gunshot wound suffered in the opening stages of the fight that destroyed flesh and bone in his arm. He was on the ground and fading in and out of consciousness due to the cumulative effects of shock and blood loss, but continued to fight back for the duration of the shoot-out. SA Mireles fired five shotgun rounds from a pump-action shotgun he had to operate with one hand, inflicting buckshot wounds on both assailants. Then he regained his feet and approached Platt and Matix as they sat in Grogan and Dove's Bureau car and ended the gunfight by shooting both in the head with his handgun. By his own account, SA Mireles was not aware of his injury until he tried to use his arm to push himself up off the ground and could not, which caused him to look at his arm and see the wound and exposed bones. By the end of the gunfight, he was functioning on sheer will and rage."[89]

In the opening days of Operation ENDURING FREEDOM in the mountains of Afghanistan, elite members of a Navy Special Mission Unit (known, variously as "Blue," SEAL Team Six or ST6) were engaged in a firefight with Taliban and AL Qaeda forces. During the firefight, members of ST6 were putting 5-6 rounds of 5.56 mm rounds fired from their heavily modified M-4 carbines into the bad guys. Much to the Blue team's surprise, the Taliban and Al Qaeda forces continued to fight for an additional 10-15 minutes, lobbing grenades and firing AK's from behind boulders. In at least one instance, one member of Blue stopped in the middle of the firefight and stared at his weapon like "How come it's not working?" These are the best of the best counter terror forces the United States possesses, yet even they are not immune to this psychological dimension to gun fighting and expectation of how bullets work. All the hard training concerning "shoot until the threat is over" that special mission unit operators go through still could not overcome the years of Hollywood and TV brainwashing that infects us all from a very young age.

Another law enforcement example involves a SWAT Team that was executing a felony arrest warrant on a known, violent armed robber in California. The SWAT team, all dressed up in their assault gear, complete with black balaclava, was ascending the stairs to the suspect's second floor apartment in preparation for a dynamic entry into the suspect's apartment.

---

[89]from In Defense of Self and Others, Urey W. Patrick and John C. Hall, Carolina Academic Press, 2005, pages 66-67

As Murphy's Law would have it, the suspect came out of the apartment early, ruining the team's element of surprise. The suspect, in fact, immediately fired down upon the team with a .44 magnum revolver. The lead SWAT Team member fell, and the rest of the team "lit up" the bad guy with submachine gun and shotgun fire, killing him in the process. The lead SWAT team member, however, was never hit: not even in the bullet resistant vest. He only thought he was shot, and his body reacted how it was preprogrammed to react when shot.

There is good news and bad news when dealing with the psychological aspects of how bullets work. Because we are fearfully and wonderfully made, the human body can withstand huge trauma and still fight and still survive, so long as we receive decent trauma care within the "golden hour." As good guys, we must always remember that and train to fight through our adversaries and our own injuries. The bad news is that the bad guys are also fearfully and wonderfully made, and in addition to their own bodies' inherent strengths, they may also bring a powerful will to the fight (as did the two subjects the FBI faced in Miami). They may also possess a strong fundamentalist religious fervor, sometimes enhanced by drug usage such as amphetamine, alcohol or pain killer abuse. Insurgents in Iraq are frequently known to come to the fight both high on amphetamines as well as with their arms pre-prepped with IV bottles to administer fluids so they don't exsanguinate as quickly.

How Bullets Work Physically

Despite all the fantasy out of Hollywood and misinformation in many gun magazines, small arms rounds[90] do not possess "knock down" or "stopping" power. Small arms projectiles physically incapacitate an individual by crushing, tearing, or destroying flesh and bone: hopefully with enough depth of penetration and permanence to either directly disrupt the body's brain-nerve function or cause enough blood volume loss to keep oxygen

---

[90]The authors are referring to handgun rounds and rifle/carbine rounds up to 7.62 NATO. It is certainly true that .50 caliber Browning Machine Gun (BMG) rounds or 12 gauge rifled slugs do possess superior "stopping" power than the aforementioned rounds, but the reality is that even these larger rounds are still governed by the general principles of wound ballistics. Once the principles of wound ballistics are grasped, it can be readily understood that projectiles which create larger and deeper holes increase the probability of timely results. However, in each case, we are still only talking about increasing probablilities.

from adequately feeding that brain-nerve function. All with a goal of stopping the bad guy from performing. Police officers, as Soldiers, really do not shoot to kill: they shoot until the threat is over. It is entirely irrelevant to the outcome of the shooting incident whether the bad guy dies. Michael Platt died, but not soon enough.

The preeminent scholar in the field of wounds ballistics, retired Army surgeon Colonel Marty Fackler, had this to say about the "shock" or "knock down power" of a small arms projectile: "The shock from being hit by a bullet is actually much like the shock from being called an idiot; it is an expression of surprise and has nothing to do with physical effects or psychological trauma."[91] The ground truth is that the amount of physical energy inflicted on the body by a small arms round is equivalent of being hit by a Major League fastball.[92]

It is impossible to accurately predict with any degree of certainty the effects of wounds created by small arms projectiles. That is why it is absurd to draft into ROE guidance such language as "use only the rounds necessary," "shoot to wound," or "shoot and assess." If a subject presents an imminent threat of death or serious bodily injury (or, in SROE parlance, presents a Hostile Act or Imminent Hostile Intent), then they are worthy of being shot until they cease to present such a threat. Shooters and ROE drafters alike must understand this concept of how bullets work, or they will continue to be subject to the other's folly.

When a bullet enters the human body it creates a temporary wound channel and a permanent wound channel. Of the two, one can only reliably count on the permanent wound channel to destroy, crush or tear flesh or bone. Even so, there is no accurate way to predict the course and effect of a small arms projectile on the human body.

Temporary Wound Channel is the larger temporary displacement of flesh or tissue caused by the transfer of energy within the body. Because we are fearfully and wonderfully made, the body has an amazing elastic quality that will absorb energy by temporarily stretching. Unless the bullet impacts close to a hard organ such as liver or spleen, this temporary stretching will cause little or no diminution of the body's ability to function. The

[91]Fackler, MI, MD, "Questions and Comments," Wound Ballistics Review, Journal of the International Wounds Ballistics Association, vol. 4(1) 1999, page 5.
[92]Hall, Id, at page 69, quoting Douglas Lindsey, MD.

tissue will simply expand then collapse back unto itself. For those familiar with the blocks of gelatin portrayed in so many gun magazines which often purport to show the "knock down" power of a particular round, the temporary wound channel is represented by the large, opaque area. Such depictions, while visually impressive, are nearly meaningless in assessing the efficacy of a particular round.

Permanent Wound Channel is the permanent path of destruction through the body caused by the passage of the projectile though flesh and bone. It is the permanent hole caused by the size, depth of penetration and course of the bullet as it traverses though the body. Many variables effect the permanent wound channel, to include, but not limited, to: velocity of the round, round fragmentation, deflection (either before or after entering the body), and size of the projectile.

Unless the permanent wound channel directly disrupts the brain-nerve function, one cannot ever assume or anticipate immediate incapacitation. The human heart can be eviscerated by a direct hit from a 7.62 mm NATO round (the standard "sniper" round within most police and military inventories) and still there will be enough oxygen in the brain for the assailant to continue to function for an additional 10-15 seconds: a seeming eternity in a firefight.

Another variable is the fact that wounds cannot be predictably relied on to bleed out in a timely fashion. Under ideal circumstances, Michael Platt's wound to his brachial artery should have drained blood from him very quickly—a 20%-25% volumic loss—causing loss of consciousness or death within seconds. Nevertheless, due to physical realities such as incomplete wounding, arterial clamping caused by adjacent tissue and muscle mass, and other unpredictable variables, Platt's will was able to overcome his injuries long enough to fight back with devastating effect on the good guys.

Part of the problem encountered by the SEAL Team in the mountains of Afghanistan was the apparent unreliability of the 5.56 mm round[93] as a close quarter's battle (CQB) weapon. Contrary to popular folklore, 5.56 rounds fired from the M-16/M-4 rifle do not "tumble" when exiting the weapon system. They spin at a high RPM just like any other Spitzer-type

---

[93] Interestingly, most states prohibit the hunting of 100 lb whitetail deer with this round because it does not create humane, immediate incapacitation in their view. Yet, the US military does not see the disconnect when it issues the same round to be fired on 180 lb human adversaries!

hunting bullet. They were designed to yaw (or go "ass over end") after achieving sufficient depth of penetration into flesh, hopefully creating a more devastating wound channel. If they do not achieve the necessary depth of penetration—in the case of many Afghan and Somali targets, the "bad guys" were simply too thin—then the round will create a "knitting needle" type injury that may not cause fast volumic blood loss. Secondly, these rounds were originally designed to be fired out of a 20" plus barrel, thereby achieving extremely high velocity with attendant bullet fragmentation on impact: all with a view of creating more grievous wound channels. When the Special Operations community (and later, Big Army) cut the original barrels down to carbine/M-4 lengths (generally 10-14 inches), they lost much of the velocity required to achieve bullet fragmentation.

1st Battalion-46th Infantry Commander observes ROE/RUF Tactical
Training Seminar at Fort Knox.

Author with members of Czech Special Operations Group (SOG) after Simunitions training in Pilzen.

Checkpoint Simunitions training at Blackwater's facility for the Navy.

COMCFSOCC, his XO, PSDNCOIC and JAG
with members of ODA 912 in Iraq.

FBI legend John C. Hall teaches at USMA, West Point
iteration of the Seminar.

Jeff Kirkham and Butch Rogers prep a stack for dynamic entry at Fort Knox.

Jim Patterson and Geoff Wilcox teaching Simunitions in Desert Scenario at the Air Mobility Warfare Center's CST Course.

Sims Action beats Reaction training scenario.

Sims Knife attack in force-on-force training scenario.

Jim Patterson teaching carbine movement at Fort Knox.

Steve Didier instructing Czech SOG.

Team member (and former SEAL and DEA Special Agent) Nick Shoemaker

CHAPTER 11

THREAT IDENTIFICATION

ABSENT CONFLICTS WHERE AMERICA'S NATIONAL LEADERSHIP has declared a force or group to be "hostile" or designate them as "enemy combatants," Soldiers, Sailors, Airmen and Marines will always be responding to a hostile act or demonstrated hostile intent (much as police officers do on a daily basis in the United States). Accordingly, it is extremely important that our service members are educated on threat identification or else face a fumble on kickoff by getting shot in the face before even recognizing that a threat exists.

Just as in evaluating the tactical dynamics of an encounter, there are lessons learned from law enforcement concerning threat identification that must be incorporated into any training regimen. The first lesson is a psychological one: human beings rarely, if ever, expect something bad to happen to them. It is always the other guy who gets into a car accident, the other family's home that is burglarized, and always the other cop who gets shot. If we were expecting to get into a gun fight, would we not bring something bigger than a pistol or rifle? It is almost a universal reaction of surprise that greets most cops involved in a deadly force encounter, even when responding to armed hold-up calls and calls where, intellectually, the officers know there is likelihood for a violent encounter.

While teaching the ROE/RUF Tactical Training Seminar at the Air Mobility Warfare Center in December 2005, the team was approached by an Army Master Sergeant assigned to the Warrior Brigade, US Army Civil

Affairs and Psychological Operations Command (USACAPOC), Fort Bragg, North Carolina. In his civilian world, this Reservist is a police officer in Arkansas. He told the cadre, then the class, of his ordeal of confronting two violent, armed robbers at a convenience store. Rolling into the store parking lot, he saw two armed men running out of the front door. As he got out of his car (or "exited his vehicle" as cops like to say!), the two men did not flee. Instead, they charged at him with their weapons blazing. This officer reported that his first reaction was one of incredulity: bad guys were supposed to run when confronted by the police. He quickly recovered his wits, retreated to the back of his vehicle, and then went into his training mode: front sites on target/trigger press. He quickly and successfully engaged both subjects multiple times with center mass hits. To his surprise, only one subject went down immediately, while the second subject hurdled his downed partner and continued to charge. The Officer quickly performed a combat reload (without hesitation and without thinking) and put more rounds into the second bad guy, hitting him with a "fatal T" shot to the brain housing group. That subject was DRT (dead right there), with his automatic pistol empty and slide locked to the rear. The Officer then shifted his attention back to the first, downed subject, who—unbelievably to the Officer—with multiple rounds center mass, was trying to push himself up off the ground to continue the attack. It took more rounds from the Officer to finally finish the job of addressing that threat. Obviously, this event shook the Officer profoundly, but he reports that it was the fact that he was twice-surprised during the event that impacted him most.

Also, we are not born pre-programmed with too much in the way of threat recognition. Nearly all of what we know is learned. While it is true that one can make a baby cry by grimacing at the child (hence, most compassionate adults will make goo-goo sounds at an infant in an attempt to make the child smile), that same child (nor most adults) would not recognize an opponent's "blading" of his body or balling of his fists as signals of an imminent attack. Yet any reasonably well-trained police officer would commit to a first strike with an asp baton on a subject if the subject exhibited such signs of a probable assault during a field interview. Neither prudence nor the law requires the law enforcement officer to take the first punch in such a situation. In fact, the officer does not even need "probable cause" (a legal threshold meaning "more likely than not") to believe an assault is imminent. The law only requires "reasonable suspicion" on the officer's part. In other words, the law does not require an officer to "gamble with his life," nor is the Constitution "a suicide pact." Members of the armed forces do not give up such Constitutional protections when they raise their right hand to defend it.

A law enforcement training model relevant to teaching Soldiers the concepts of threat identification—I.e., when one is confronted with an individual or group that has demonstrated the (1) hostile intent, (2) ability and (3) opportunity to inflict death or grievous bodily injury upon yourself or innocent others—is the threat triangle:

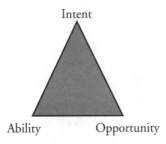

Intent

Woody Allen once remarked that he was expelled from a philosophy exam because he was caught "peering into the soul" of the girl next to him. We do not need to perform such clairvoyant maneuvers to divine hostile intent. In fact, a suspect's subjective intent, legally and tactically, is not at all relevant. An insane person, or someone highly intoxicated on drugs or alcohol, may possess very little ability to formulate subjective hostile intent. Or, as John Hall is fond of quoting, "Very little mentation is required for deadly action. A rattlesnake is deadly but could not form the mental state required for conviction of murder."

Rather, we should be training Soldiers as we train cops: to recognize "objective" hostile intent. Many lessons can be gleaned from the law enforcement experience in identifying such intent. These lessons are applicable across the mission spectrum of the military: from humanitarian relief missions to force on force conflict.

Pre-Assaultive Behaviors.

Individuals (other than when striking from a hidden ambush position) generally do not initiate a violent act without first exhibiting certain pre-assaultive behaviors (or "clues" as we like to say in law enforcement settings!). In other words, a trained law enforcement officer will be attuned to the body language—such as the aforementioned "blading" of the body or balling of the fists—that often occur before an offensive action is undertaken by an suspect. Some other pre-assaultive behaviors are: anger or determination in the facial mien; pacing, puffing out of the chest; and, strutting or actual bull-like pawing of the earth with one's feet. Tony Lambraia, a senior tactical instructor at the Federal Law Enforcement Training Center (FLETC) in Glynco, Georgia, jokingly states, "In New York, it takes 20 minutes of 'No, fuck YOU' before the first punch is thrown!"

Perhaps the most prevalent pre-assaultive behavior threat indicator is "verbal noncompliance." If a uniformed, armed police officer (or Soldier) is pointing a weapon at you, yelling "Freeze" or "Halt," that is a hint. Most reasonable people, regardless of whether the verbal warning was in a foreign language, would be prudent to follow such direction. It should not be a surprise to an individual if they are shot after openly disobeying a cop or Soldier who is pointing a weapon and ordering "freeze" or "halt." If a suspect starts playing "stupid" (as in "what me?") or, instead, ignores the command completely, then that behavior should immediately be seen as a danger sign to the cop or Soldier that something bad might happen. Under certain circumstances, such as when a suspect ignores a command to "drop the knife" or "keep your hands where I can see them," the verbal noncompliance might be an immediate predicate to deadly force. Under those circumstances, at the very minimum, the verbal noncompliance of a subject should place the officer or Soldier in a heightened state of alertness and awareness that something may be awry.

Watch the hands.

More than any other part of the human body, the hands of a suspect are constantly a concern for most prudent law enforcement officers. The mouth may be running, or the eyes batting, but it is the hands that will most likely access the weapon or initiate the assault upon the suspect's intended victim. That is why verbal noncompliance by a potentially armed suspect to a command "show me your hands" must be viewed as a sign of demonstrated hostile intent or imminent hostile act. Under such circumstances, officers would be foolhardy to wait to see a weapon before taking immediate action.

Multiple Subjects (or Assailants).

More than one suspect or assailant also dramatically increases the danger to a Soldier or law enforcement officer. Despite such Hollywood antics showing cops (or martial arts experts) fending off two, three or more attackers, the advantage a group has over an individual is high and the odds are not in favor of the individual no matter how skilled a fighter he may be. This is true even though the officer or Soldier may possess the only firearm on the scene. In addition to the sheer physical advantage multiple assailants will possess over the individual cop or Soldier, multiple assailants are also danger due to the aforementioned tunnel vision dynamic that comes into play. In other words, the Soldier or cop may be so distracted by an "obvious" bad guy (either an actual or feigned threat), that they will exclude or not focus on other possible threats within the group until it is too late.

Soldiers are often faced with this dilemma at traffic control points and entry control points. That is why it is critical that there be sufficient personnel present, and hopefully in an "overwatch" position with a clear field of fire, to attenuate this problem. But, out on patrol or conducting peace-enforcing missions, Soldiers may not have that luxury. They need to be trained on threat identification and recognize that a hostile crowd—even if apparently "unarmed"—can still present a very serious threat. If the mission allows, it may be prudent for the patrol to quickly exfiltrate from an area to avoid a potentially ugly and uneven situation. But the Soldiers have to first be trained on recognizing the problem before seeking solutions.

Enemy Tactics Techniques and Procedures

The previously utilized tactics, techniques and procedures (TTPs) the enemy has used before can be a huge building block in the development of assessing hostile intent. If the enemy has been known to use an injured civilian as a ruse to stop a convoy or divert the attention of a patrol, should that situation arise again, the patrol would be wise to go into "condition yellow" real quick…in other words be really switched on and wary to attack.

Theater-Specific Intelligence

Lastly, so long as it is efficiently and accurately pumped down to the lowest tactical levels, theater-specific intelligence can also be used as a building block to divining intent. Law enforcement lawfully and reasonably relies on similar reports all the time. For instance, if a cop receives an "all points bulletin" (APB) or "be on the lookout" for a violent and armed criminal suspect, and then that cop performs a car stop on a vehicle and driver matching the description of that APB, the officer would be smart (and within his legal rights) to treat that situation as a "felony car stop." In other words, the officer should safely remove the individual at gunpoint from the vehicle. If the driver, known to fit the description of an armed and violent felon, disregards the officer's commands, the officer may be prudent to engage that subject even before ever seeing a weapon. The law allows the officer to rely on police communications and "intelligence" concerning that individual. Similarly, if a Soldier possesses information gleaned from US or Coalition intelligence sources, the Soldier should reasonably be able to rely on such information when developing an immediate threat assessment of possible hostile intent.

Ability

Sadly, most civilians (and, it appears, judge advocates) gain their knowledge concerning the ability of an adversary to inflict death or grievous bodily injury from Hollywood. How else would one explain such insanity currently extant in many modern-day ROE such as "use minimum force," "use proportionate force," "exhaust lesser means," or "don't load a round into the chamber until confronted with an imminent threat?"

The best example of this misunderstanding can be found when law enforcement officers confront an individual armed with an edged weapon. Most people unskilled or uneducated in such matters become upset when a cop or group of cops shoots a suspect armed "only with a knife," and sometimes from seemingly "safe" distances. Immediately, the caterwauling from the civil rights groups and media begins. Some ask, "Why didn't the officers 'swarm' the suspect, there were four cops and only one bad guy?" Ignoring the obvious question—"Who wants to be the first 'Swarmee?'"— such Monday morning quarter backing ignores the ability of an individual armed with an edged weapon to inflict death or grievous bodily injury on a group thirty feet away armed with firearms. Again, most hearken back to the image from the Indiana Jones movie where "Indy" shoots dead a scimitar wielding assailant who "only" brought a knife to a gunfight. While a cute movie ploy, the scene inaccurately represents the true threat an individual with an edged weapon presents. In a real-world scenario, Indy would stand a very good chance of getting cut badly, if not killed, by the assailant.

But, the realities of wound ballistics, action-versus-reaction, and the fact that law enforcement officers miss approximately 80% of the time during actual engagements, will tilt the scales in favor of the assailant. Law enforcement officers are trained on these realities and that is why prudence and the law allows them to engage. It should NEVER be a fair or "proportionate"[2] fight.

It is common knowledge amongst trained law enforcement officers that a suspect armed with an edged weapon thirty feet away presents a deadly threat. This is because an average suspect can close that distance in less than two seconds, while the officer will take nearly that amount of time to recognize danger, draw and point his weapon, and then pull the trigger. Then, assuming everything works in the officer's favor—he accurately fires, hits the suspect; the bullet strikes and immediately impairs the brain-nerve function—the edged weapon may still strike and cut the officer due to the suspect's momentum.

Even if the officer fires two shots and gets good, center mass hits with both of them, the suspect may still have enough oxygen in his brain

---

[2] It is amazing how many judge advocates incorrectly infuse the law of armed conflict (LOAC) principle of "proportionality" into tactical ROE concerning rules for the use of deadly force. "Proportionality" in LOAC terms simply means that in military operations force should be proportionate to a threat in order to avoid unnecessary civilian causalities or collateral damage. In other words, don't drop a 2,000 pound bomb in the middle of a crowded marketplace in order to take out one enemy combatant. Proportionality has zero to do with how one should respond with small arms to a hostile act or demonstrated hostile intent. Yet, too many times ROE/RUF is infused with this concept—"the force used must be proportional to the threat" (Operation JUMP START, June 2, 2006, rules for force for National Guardsmen on the Southwest Border)—implying that somehow confrontations with a hostile actor must be "fair."

housing group and adrenaline in his system to keep attacking for another five to ten seconds. The officer can increase his odds by shooting on the move and moving laterally, but this assumes that these skill sets have been taught (which is a faulty assumption in light of most military firearms qualification courses) and practiced under high stress conditions. Five to ten seconds of a still-armed assailant cutting, stabbing and slashing, all the while the office is left to defend himself "close in" with a handgun. The officer can continue shooting and hope that the suspect bleeds out more quickly or a round hits an area that will immediately disable the brain-nerve function, but the situation will be dangerous, violent and bloody.

So, our Soldiers must be trained to recognize the fact that an insurgent with a machete (or baseball bat or paving stone) as distant as thirty feet or more may present an imminent threat of death or grievous bodily injury. This doesn't mean that they must shoot all such threats, but rather that any decision on their part NOT to shoot such a subject should be a knowing and intelligent decision.

Opportunity

In the same knife wielding situation described above, if one were to place twelve foot chain link fence between the assailant and the officer, the opportunity would vanish. Much of the opportunity concept is situational-dependent and the "threat triangle" is a constantly moving and morphing concept—not subject to written rules or restrictions. That is why folks placed into situations where they must make decisions concerning the application of deadly force must be trained on threat recognition and judgment and not hampered with legally overly-restrictive and confusing rules and matrices concerning the use of force.

Too often, I am confronted by critics of the ROE/RUF Tactical Training Seminar (mostly from individuals who have never been though the course) that imply that law enforcement training is irrelevant to military mission or, worse, that we are teaching Soldiers to be "trigger happy." Such critiques are misplaced for any number of reasons, but primarily because (1) the SROE mandates that commanders at all levels instruct their subordinates on appropriate threat recognition and self-defense response and (2) the realities of law enforcement belie such concerns. In any given year over the past decade, an average of 66,000 law enforcement officers were assaulted. Of those assaults, over 16,500 were with a dangerous and deadly weapon (where, as a matter of law, deadly force would be authorized). Yet, law enforcement only shot 800 subjects into the ground during that same time period.

CHAPTER 12

THE SAFETY TAIL WAGS THE DOG...HOW AMERICA MAY LOSE ITS COUNTER-INSURGENCIES

BILAD, IRAQ. EARLY 2006. A member of one of America's Special Forces units just came off mission and was heading to the Base Exchange. A military policeman stopped this warrior as he attempted to enter the exchange. The following Catch-22esque colloquy ensued:

"You can't come in, Sergeant," intoned the MP.

"Why not?"

"Because you aren't wearing a reflective safety belt, and the base commander has ordered that all personnel must wear a reflective safety belt 24/7 while on base," answered the MP.

"I know, " replied the warrior, "that's why I am here, to buy a safety belt."

"But you can't come in without a safety belt...that's the Colonel's orders...sorry Sarge." The operator left without a belt or sundries, no doubt wondering how much more perverse the Safety Nazis could become.

If this were a one-time example of an overzealous and overly cautious senior leader in our military, there would be no cause for alarm. Unfortunately, however, it is quickly becoming the norm:

One can barely maneuver around an American-controlled base Iraq or

Afghanistan without tripping over "clearing barrels" emplaced because of the paralyzing and generally unwarranted obsession in the military over accidental or "negligent" discharges. Unwarranted, because comprehensive and realistic training would correct such deficiencies. 200,000 police officers walk around the streets of America with loaded and holstered weapons, generally without a problem. In war zones, however, Soldiers coming back onto base—regardless of their age, rank or level of experience (to include the aforementioned Special Forces professional)—must remove their safely holstered weapons from the holster, manipulate them in a crowded area, and "clear" (unload) them with barrels pointed into the sand-filled clearing barrels. And when a weapon does, on occasion, fire into a clearing barrel (Isn't that why they have clearing barrels?), the command generally crucifies the guilty party.

This panic has gotten so bad that a Command Sergeant Major from a Special Forces unit recently reported that he knows of some senior leaders that "fake" charging their weapons when they go outside the wire so that they avoid the potential for an accidental discharge upon their return to base. There have also been many reports of military members being forced to place strips of colored tape over their magazine wells to visually demonstrate that their weapons are unloaded. A group that calls itself the "Armed Forces" has gradually and consistently developed a fear and vilification of weapons to rival Disney movies. Oh, and never mind that an unloaded weapon in a war zone is about as effective as a coat hangar in fighting off the bad guys.

On any given day, one can observe Sergeants Major (the highest enlisted rank in the military) standing on street corners on bases in Iraq checking to see if the drivers of passing military vehicles are wearing seatbelts on streets already hamstrung by 15 mph speed limits. Besides being laughable, this is hardly an efficient use of experienced military leaders, who are supposed to be advising general and field grade officers on the conduct of the mission and effectiveness of their fighting force.

Here at training bases in the United States, realistic firearms' training is consistently stymied due to "safety concerns." Soldiers, Sailors, Airmen and Marines—except those assigned to so-called "Tier One" units—rarely, if ever, are allowed to practice "shoot on the move" techniques, combat reloads, or other tactical engagement scenarios due to overzealous safety concerns. Anyone who has ever shot on a military range has heard the constant range control mantra of "Keep your weapons pointed up and downrange, don't load until directed by the tower, etc.," forgetting all the time that there is no "up and downrange" in Iraq. More importantly, the enemy is never a readily identifiable static target just waiting to be shot on command.

Attempts to introduce innovative and realistic training methodologies like the use of Simunitions (non-lethal training ammunition—essentially glorified paint balls—fired from the Soldiers' weapons that can deliver effective threat identification and tactical training) or shoot on the move live-fire techniques is most often met with stiff resistance or outright nay saying by those in command or in charge of range control. Such effective training is only allowed to proceed when senior leaders who are not prone to risk averse thinking become aware of the problem and wade in to correct it

Some officers and noncommissioned officers have made careers out of becoming "Safety Officers." Monthly magazines are published in all four services with myriad new checklists and safety methodologies. It has gotten so bad that one can't run innovative and more realistic weapons training without running afoul of the latest nonsense. This type of "safety first" mentality is indicative of America's having bred an entire generation of risk-averse officers. This is dangerous because it is contrary to developing a warrior mentality and it degrades realistic training.

The risk-averse atmosphere has created a military where safety isn't merely an aspect of the mission, but rather has become the mission. Training, development, and, sadly, even tactics are often subordinated to "safety." It shouldn't be "safety first," it should be "mission first, as safe as reasonably possible." Otherwise, Insurgents—unconcerned about whether their rifles have been properly cleared—will drag too many reflective safety belt-adorned American bodies down the street.

CHAPTER 13

THE SOLUTION:
COMBAT-FOCUSED TRAINING

A NUMBER OF JUDGE ADVOCATES AND TACTICAL WEAPONS INSTRUCTORS, tired of the ineffective "ROE Briefings" and static weapons qualification courses, collaborated to develop the Rules of Engagement(ROE)/Rules for the Use of Force(RUF) Tactical Training Seminar. Since 2000, this course has been taught at several locations, to include: Special Operations Command Central, MacDill AFB; Fort Jackson, South Carolina; the FBI Academy, Quantico, Virginia; United States Military Academy, West Point, New York; 1st Armored Training Brigade, Fort Knox, Kentucky; the SIGArms Academy, Exeter, New Hampshire; and, to the Czech Special Operations Group in Pilzen. These sessions familiarized commanders, operational personnel, legal advisors, and trainers from DOD, DOJ, and other federal, state, local and allied agencies concerning the application of force, particularly deadly force.

These two and one-half day seminars provide a detailed overview on the law, wound ballistics and bullet performance (how and what bullets do to stop an adversary), and the psycho-physiological reactions of humans under high stress tactical environments and shooting situations. These briefings are followed by at least two full days of practical exercises using either the Firearms Training System (FATS) or Engagement Skill Trainer

(EST), both being scenario driven video based threat recognition and judgment training.

By using these interactive, scenario-driven, video-based judgment training devices, students experience rapidly evolving deadly force judgment scenarios, where they encounter innocent civilians, friendly forces, and "bad guys," identifiable as such only by their actions. Students assess behavior, determine whether a threat exists, and react appropriately. The system also helps reinforce bedrock deadly force principles, such as "keep shooting until the threat has ended," rather than tactically unrealistic but familiar ROE card guidance such as "shoot to kill," or "stop firing as soon as the situation permits." The firearms used in FATS are usually real duty firearms, driven by an air charge that causes recoil and the slide to operate. FATS weapons are limited to real ammunition capacity and must be tactically reloaded during a firefight. The system also records hits, misses, as well as distinguishing between potentially lethal hits and probable wounds. This system is also a superb device to train another bedrock principal, that of "action beats reaction" every time. Soldiers often mistakenly carry their weapons in a fashion that would prohibit them from reacting quickly enough to save their lives during a realistic encounter. Deadly threats are rarely as clear as they seem during traditional ROE training.

By undergoing force-on-force training using Simunitions (the aforementioned plastic paint rounds fired at 450' per second from duty weapons), defensive tactics and advanced reflexive shooting marksmanship training, participants experience the stress of a deadly encounter by engaging "bad guy" role players using firearms that shoot plastic, dye-filled projectiles. A bad guy/potential threat role player/s, often similarly armed, is encountered, a shoot-no shoot judgment must be made, and trainees must react and eliminate the threat, or in some cases, not shoot. The projectiles provide realistic recoil, point of aim, and noise. The projectiles can sting when they strike, but cause no permanent injury. This provides training otherwise unavailable that clearly displays how fast such encounters occur and how little time is really available for a decision. This trains all personnel, particularly attorneys, to draft simple, realistic rules. It becomes immediately apparent to even the most academic personalities that applying complex, wordy, and convoluted ROE is simply impossible in realistic encounters.

Such force-on-force training also provides a level of "stress inoculation" against some of the more deadly aspects of the Tache-Psyche effect. Dave Grossman analogizes this to how we overcome fear in other aspects of our lives: by doing it repeatedly!

Expert instructors from various military departments, law enforcement agencies, civilian experts, and legal instructors, provide the classroom instruction. Later, students viscerally experience the phenomena and issues discussed in the classroom setting while using FATS, Simunitions, or on the range. This combination of practical, tactical training with legal instruction has proven very successful when employed by federal law enforcement agencies and military Special Mission Units.

Frequently in the Army and Air Force, "training" is checked off for individuals receiving legal briefings on ROE, given by the JAG, and firearms qualification, where operational trainers ensure that personnel are "qualified" with their assigned weapon (meet some minimum standard sometimes wholly unrelated to actual combat shooting). Neither type of training adequately prepares personnel for decision making under stress, nor do they always provide realistic shooting training. DOJ has found that combining the legal and tactical elements, while contrary to the "stay in your lane" specialization mentality, provides the best results in both areas.

In the ROE/RUF Tactical Training Seminar, instructors from various military and civilian law enforcement units present a series of hands-on dynamic and interactive training exercises allowing attendees to experience the phenomena of a high stress tactical environment.

This tactical training allows the operators to internalize the interrelationship between ROE/RUF and the tactical realities of force encounters. This enhanced understanding will better tactically, legally and mentally prepare military service members to properly apply the reasonable amount force, to include deadly force, to defend themselves and affect the mission when faced with a hostile actor or a declared hostile.

Using Non-Lethal Training Ammunitions (NLTA), like Simunitions (which is a brand-name) operators are able to use their own weapons and targeting skills to engage potential hostiles armed with firearms, knives, and other weapons, or in hand-to-hand confrontations. These situational exercises and training opportunities transcend traditional firearms and defensive tactics training. The program provides the operators with essential information regarding the use of force and with "holistic" knowledge and practical applications in the use of force. This understanding cultivates operator empowerment and proper judgment by allowing the fluid integration of decision-making and tactical concerns. Very simply, confidence of Use of Force authority and skill leads to operator competence.

Weapons Qualifications: Time to Rethink Static Targets.

An exploration of the various services' individual weapons qualifications doctrines reveals serious shortcomings, even for those serving in combat units. Of great concern is the dangerously inadequate marksmanship requirement for combat support personnel. By way of example, in the Army, Category II (all non-Infantry, Combat Engineer or Military Police personnel) Soldiers are expected to zero with 18 rounds; practice fire with 40 rounds; record fire with 40 rounds; NBC practice with 20 rounds; NBC record fire with 20 rounds; night practice with 20 rounds; and, night qualify with 20 rounds.[3] Annually, then, Soldiers will meet their training requirement by shooting a total of 178 rounds of 5.56 mm ball ammunition at stationary targets that are not firing back at them. Often times, especially for Reserve and Guard forces, even this meager annual requirement is not met.

Recognizing that its support personnel have had insufficient weapons training; the Army recently began to change its methodology for apportionment so that those assigned to combat units receive the same amount of ammunition as their combat arms brethren. There has been, however, no substantial change to the methodology by which Soldiers are trained. With the exception of some recently mandated convoy live-fire exercises and marginal changes to the marksmanship strategy in its Initial Entry Training (IET), the Army has simply doubled the ammunition allocated toward the same type of sterile, static training that is has previously been conducted.

All Soldiers, Sailors, Airmen and Marines deploying to combat zones—regardless of their specialty—should undergo rigorous tactical training[4], to include: shooting on the move, immediate action drills

---

[3] Department of the Army Pamphlet 350-38, Standards in Weapons Training, Chapter 5 (3 July 1997).
[4] See also, Master Chief Torpedoman's Mate M.R. Vimislik's comment and discussion in Proceedings, August 2004, at p.12.

(mounted and dismounted), defensive tactics, and realistic STX. Service members need to experience a full training progression from static (weapon familiarization and marksmanship) to dynamic (combat reloading and shoot on the move) to inter-active (STX).

Threat Assessments: What Are the Bad Guys Doing?

In his book *American Soldier,* General Tommy Franks laments that National Security Counsel Counter-terror expert Richard Clarke provided him "no actionable intelligence" concerning Al Qaeda at critical junctures during Operation Enduring Freedom. General Frank's frustration is shared at a unit level on a daily basis by combat support and combat service support service members deploying into hostile fire zones. Often, these troops arrive at an airfield during evening hours, are hustled into transport vehicles, and placed into a convoy to their assigned duty location. They ride off without a clear understanding of the route, security in place, potential hostiles, or what to do if attacked.

Before any convoy operation, in addition to rehearsing vehicle battle drills and performing pre-combat checks, all participants should, at a minimum, have a clear understanding of the following:

- Radio call signs, frequencies, and medical evacuation (MEDEVAC) procedures;
- How to call for Quick Reaction Force (QRF) assistance;
- Route of travel and alternate routes of travel; and
- Up-to-date ROE and reminder of their inherent right of self-defense.

Lastly, the latest intelligence briefings concerning threat identification and the techniques, tactics, and procedures the enemy is using in the region need to be provided to the lowest levels. The bad guys are not wearing Al Qaeda T-shirts, so each service member must be regularly trained on threat recognition. Absent a clearly defined hostile force, coalition forces are often behind the action-reaction power curve.

Devote More Energy To Little Stuff…Like Combat-Focused Training!

Much has been made recently concerning deficiencies of appropriate tactical equipment necessary to safely negotiate today's hostile fire zones. The fact remains that if service members do not possess the fundamental ability to observe, orient, decide, and act appropriately against a perceived threat and, as importantly, a clear understanding of their legal authority to do so, all the fancy equipment in the world will not save lives. Amateurs love talking about military equipment and hardware. Professional warriors are much more interested in skills, mindset or "software." When asked his views on a new pistol that the FBI was considering for adoption by its Special Agents, a former FBI Academy tactical instructor remarked, "You can't fix a pig!" He was not talking about the weapon, but rather the lack of combat-focused training provided to the new agents.

True combat-focused training, however, can "fix the pig" and can save lives more than any new piece of hardware. Not every target that presents itself is hostile and not every situation requires deadly force. Moreover, true combat-focused training should incorporate battlefield stressors that flex service members' cognitively, emotionally, environmentally, and physiologically.

An example of such training that has been successfully implemented by a number of Active Duty and Reserve Force units is the ROE/RUF Tactical Training Seminar. This session familiarizes military attendees with the legal and tactical lessons learned by the U.S. Department of Justice (DOJ) and the civilian law enforcement community concerning the application of use of force—especially deadly force. The classroom sessions focus on wound ballistics, the law, and the psycho-physiological reactions to high stress tactical environments. In the tactical training sessions, instructors from various military and police units present a series of hands-on, realistic and relevant STXs, which allow attendees to experience the phenomena of a high stress tactical environment.

The seminar combines a morning briefing on the law, wound ballistics (how and what bullets do to stop an adversary), and the psycho-physiological reactions under high stress tactical environments and shooting situations with two full days of static, dynamic and interactive practical exercises. The dynamic instruction includes defensive tactics and advanced reflexive shooting marksmanship training. The interactive exercises utilize the Firearms Training System (FATS), a scenario-driven video system that train threat recognition and judgment, similar to the Army's Engagement

Skills Trainer (EST) and force-on-force training using Simunitions (plastic, dye-filled rounds fired safely from duty weapons).

Throughout both the dynamic and interactive training regimens, the students experience rapidly evolving deadly force judgment scenarios, where they encounter innocent civilians, friendly forces, and "bad guys," identifiable as such only by their actions. Students assess the potential hostile actor's behavior, determine whether a threat exists, and learn to react appropriately. The training also helps reinforce bedrock deadly force principles, such as "keep shooting until the threat has ended," rather than tactically unrealistic but familiar ROE card guidance such as "shoot to wound," or "stop firing as soon as the situation permits."

Students are forced to rely upon near-instantaneous judgment—judgment that can *only* be gained by exposing the student to a variety of complex situations requiring immediate detection, decision, and reaction. Students learn to make these judgments after receiving a legal foundation on use of deadly force citing situations the law already recognizes in *Graham v. Connor*, 490 U.S. 386 (1989), and earlier common law cases such as *Brown v. United States*, 41 S.Ct. 501, 502 (1921), which states, "Detached reflection cannot be demanded in the presence of an uplifted knife." Such legal authority is ubiquitous throughout American, English and most civilized nations' body of jurisprudence...all having roots in the recognition of the right of self-defense. Why, then, are we demanding detached reflection in the presence of an uplifted AK-47?

In an attempt to answer this question, the seminar's classroom briefings debunk many legal and tactical myths concerning this issue. So, in addition to imparting very valuable, easily taught and understood tactical skills, the seminar's legal focus is on educating commanders and Judge Advocates and other attendees on the law as it relates to using force in self-defense.

This combining of practical, tactical training with legal instruction has proven very successful when employed by federal law enforcement agencies and military Special Mission Units. Frequently in the Army and Air Force, legal "training" is checked off for individuals receiving legal briefings on ROE, given by the JAG, and "tactical" training is checked off by firearms qualification, where operational trainers ensure that personnel are "qualified" with their assigned weapon. Neither type of training adequately prepares personnel for decision making under stress, nor do they always provide realistic shooting training. DOJ has found that combining the legal and tactical elements, while contrary to the "stay in your lane" specialization mentality, provides the best results in both areas. Units' Operational Trainers and Judge Advocates must work together to quickly incorporate this lesson into military training methodologies.

Lastly, the seminar directly confronts a philosophical change that has occurred over the past four decades concerning attitudes towards weapons and weapons systems. For an entity that calls itself "the Armed Forces," most U.S. military members never develop an intimate and close relationship with firearms. Often to the contrary, service members are taught to fear rather than become masters of their individual weapons. Such fearful attitudes, often the result of Hollywood and media engendered misperceptions about firearms, are reinforced from first-time experiences at Initial Military Training ranges. ROE/RUF Tactical Training Seminar instructors often spend hours assisting students in overcoming this learned fear.

Special Mission Unit operators routinely fire upwards to 500 rounds of small arms ammunition per week. While such ammunition expenditures are clearly not practical or necessary for others, the military needs to increase the amount of ammunition available for every Soldier, Sailor, Airman, and Marine, especially those with a potential to deploy to a hostile fire zone. Until the industrial base can meet the needs of the total force, commanders can—with a little imagination and the force of will—come very close to the live-fire experience using such tools as the Engagement Skills Trainer (EST), Laser-Convoy Counter Ambush Training System (L-CCATS), paintball guns, and Simunitions. The latter two are low-cost supplements to live-fire training that enable realistic judgment-based training and enhance individual weapons skills.

Commanders and Soldiers/Airmen are always looking for simple, direct, and easily applied ROE/RUF that answer their fundamental use of force question, "When can I pull the trigger?" While general guidelines for upper command levels can be set forth in the ROE/RUF in an Operations Order (OPORD), and even more particularized guidance handed out on ROE Cards, the answer to such a question is almost always incident specific and must be based on the split second judgment of individual Soldiers on the scene. Such <u>judgment-based training</u> is the opposite of the usual <u>rules-based training</u> individuals receive in this area. As a further benefit, this judgment-based training in no way degrades traditional force-on-force combat skills, but rather it enhances them. To assist any command interested in adopting this training, Appendix B contains a detailed Program of Instruction (POI) and course schedule for the Seminar. One caveat, however: make sure that "switched-on" instructors with both the tactical and legal experience and skills are teaching it.

Lastly, there may be light at the end of the tunnel. At the time of this book's publication, both the Army's 1st Armor Training Brigade at Fort Knox (an Army Training and Doctrine Command unit) and the Navy's Expeditionary Combat Command at Little Creek are actively investigating the infusion of this training concept into their respective doctrines concerning escalation of force training.

APPENDIX

RULES OF ENGAGEMENT
RULES FOR THE USE OF FORCE
TACTICAL TRAINING SEMINAR

COURSE LESSON PLAN

ROE/RUF
TRAINING DIRECTORATE

ONE DAY COMPRESSED DV and
THREE DAY COURSE SCHEDULE

Day 1	Admin & Logistics Support Day			
Time	Event	Who	Location	POC
0800 – 1130	Safety Overview, Assignment Overview, Logistics, Admin, etc. Range Safety brief	Instructors		
0900-1000	FATS/EST scenario review/facilities tour	Instructors		
1130-1230	Lunch	Instructors		
1300-1600	Facilities tour (pistol, carbine range and training platform site survey)	Instructors		
1300-1600	Use of Force Legal and Tactical Realities Briefing	All Students that have not seen the brief		

Day 2	One-Day Compressed DV Course [Ammo drop: 1,500 rds 9mm; 1,000 rds 5.56 mm; 1,000 rds Sims FX Marking]			
Time	Event	Who	Location	POC
0730	Weapon, safety gear issue	Instructors		
0800-0830	Welcome, Admin & Range Safety Brief	All		
0830-1015	M-9 Pistol	DV Students	Range	
	M-4 Long Gun	Group 2	Range	
1015-1200	M-4 Long Gun	DV Students	Range	
	M-9 Pistol	Group 2	Range	
1200-1300	Lunch (catered event)	All	Chow Hall or Field	
1330-1445	Scenarios [Sims FX Marking]	All DV Students		
1515-1630	FATS/EST	All DV Students	FATS/EST facility	
	Wrap-up	All		
1645-1730	Weapon cleaning/return Hot wash/Day 3 Review	Instructors		1

Day 3	ROE/RUF TTS (Day 1) [Ammo drop: 8,000 rds 9mm; 6,000 rds 5.56 mm]			
Time	Event	Who	Location	POC
0730	Weapon, safety gear issue	Instructors	Range	
0730-0800	Welcome, Admin & Range Safety Brief	All Students		
0800-1200	M-9 Pistol	Group 1		
	M-4 Long Gun	Group 2		
1200-1230	Lunch	All		
1230-1630	M-4 Long Gun	Group 1		
	M-9 Pistol	Group 2		
1630-1700	Weapon cleaning/return Hot wash/Day 4 Review	Instructors/ Students		

Day 4	ROE/RUF TTS (Day 2) [Ammo drop: 6,000 rds 9mm; 3,000 rds 5.56]			
Time	Event	Who	Location	POC
0700	Weapon, safety gear issue	Instructors		
0730-0930	M-9 Pistol (Advanced)	Group 1		
	M-4 Long Gun (Advanced)	Group 2		
0930-1130	M-4 Long Gun (Advanced)	Group 1		
	M-9 Pistol (Advanced)	Group 2		
1130-1230	Transport to CSF NW & Lunch	All		
1230-1430	FATS	Group 1		
	M-9 Pistol (Advanced – Cont'd)	Group 2		
1430-1630	M-9 Pistol (Advanced – Cont'd)	Group 1		
	FATS	Group 2		
1630-1700	Weapon cleaning/return Hot wash/Day 5 Review	Instructors		

Day 5	ROE/RUF TTS (Day 3) [Ammo drop: 6,000 rds Sims FX Marking]			
Time	Event	Who	Location	POC
0700	Sim weapon, safety gear and tactical gear issue	Instructors		
0730-0930	Sims Decision Drills – 30 ft rule, etc. [Sims FX Marking]	Group 1		
	Checkpoint Scenarios [Sims FX Marking]	Group 2		
0930-1130	Checkpoint Scenarios [Sims FX Marking]	Group 1		
	Sims Decision Drills – 30 ft rule, etc. [Sims FX Marking]	Group 2		
1130-1230	Lunch	All		
1230-1430	Final Exercises – Simunitions [Sims FX Marking]	All		
1430-1500	Course Wrap-up	All		
1500-1530	Sim weapon cleaning/return	Instructors		

SYLLABUS FOR 5 DAY COURSE

Day 1	Admin & Logistics Support Day			
Time	Event	Who	Location	POC
0800 – 1130	Safety Overview, Assignment Overview, Logistics, Admin, etc. Range Safety brief	Instructors		
0900-1000	FATS/EST scenario review/facilities tour	Instructors		
1130-1230	Lunch	Instructors		
1300-1600	Facilities tour (pistol, carbine range and Navy training platform site survey)	Instructors		
1300-1600	Use of Force Legal and Tactical Realities Briefing	All Students that have not seen the brief		

Day 2				
Time	Event	Who	Location	POC
0730-0800	Introduction to EST/FATS	All		
0800-1000	EST/FATS	All		
1000-1200	Detention Techniques/Combatives	All		
1200-1315	LUNCH	All		
1315-1515	Group 1: M9 Pistol Dry Fire	Pistol Instructors		
	Group 1: M4 Carbine Dry Fire	Carbine Instructors		
	Group 1: M4 Carbine Dry Fire	Carbine Instructors		
1515-1715	Group 2: M9 Pistol Dry Fire	Pistol Instructors		
1715-1800	Instructor De-Brief (AAR)	All Instructors		

Day 3	AMMO: ____ 9mm, ____ 5.56mm per student			
Time	Event	Who	Location	POC
0730-0800	Transition to Range	All		
0800-1200	Group 1: M9 Pistol	Pistol Instructors		
	Group 2: M4 Carbine	Carbine Instructors		
1230-1300	LUNCH	All		
1300-1730	Group 1: M9 Pistol	Pistol Instructors		
	Group 2: M4 Carbine	Carbine Instructors		
1730-1800	Instructor De-Brief (AAR)	Instructors		

Day 4	AMMO: ____ 9mm, ____ 5.56mm per student			
Time	Event	Who	Location	POC
0730-0800	Transition to Range	All		
0800-1230	Group 1: M4 Carbine	Carbine Instructors		
	Group 2: M9 Pistol	Pistol Instructors		
1230-1300	LUNCH			
1300-1730	Group 1: M4 Carbine	Carbine Instructors		
	Group 2: M9 Pistol	Pistol Instructors		
1730-1800	Instructor De-Brief (AAR)	All Instructors		

Day 5	____ rnds FX Marking per student / instructor			
Time	Event	Who	Location	POC
0700-0730	Transition to MOUT	All		
0730-0900	FX Safety Brief/30-ft Rule and Action-Reaction Demos	All		
0900-1200	Group 1: Room Clearing			
	Group 2: ECP/TCP			
1200-1300	LUNCH	All		
1300-1600	Group 1: ECP/TCP			
	Group 2: Room Clearing			
1600-1700	Hotwash (AAR) and Graduation	All		

DESCRIPTION OF COURSE:

This course provides military personnel with an understanding of legal and tactical application of the Rules of Engagement and Rules for the Use of Force to self-defense situations. It also discusses basic concepts in weapon manipulation, simulated force on force exercises, force on force scenario training, and judgment-based decision making. The program material is presented via classroom, range, MOUT (w/non-lethal training ammunition), and Engagement Skills Trainer (EST) or Firearms Training Systems (FATS) instruction.

TERMINAL LEARNING OBJECTIVE (TLO):

Given a live scenario, the student will demonstrate the ability to make a rapid and legally correct use of force judgment and , if appropriate, engage in the timely and effective use of deadly force The student will then demonstrate the ability to describe the reasons behind the decision that was made and defend his actions

ENABLING LEARNING OBJECTIVES (ELO):

ELO#1: Identify concepts or principles that enable the students to develop the ability to make "objectively reasonable" decisions.

ELO#2: Identify factors that affect an student's mental preparation.

ELO#3: Identify triggers of the sympathetic nervous system and the associated negative effects.

ELO#4: Identify the legal standards for use of deadly force in self defense.

ELO#5: Successfully operate the basic weapons systems (M9, M4) in order to prepare for and conduct range based live fire judgment shooting drills and scenario based force on force simunitions training.

ELO#6: Identify pre-incident and pre-assaultive indicators that enable the students to properly assess a potential threat.

ELO#7: Prepare students to articulate the facts and circumstances justifying use of deadly force in self defense.

INSTRUCTOR GUIDE METHODOLOGIES:

Legal Presentation- sets focus of the course and 'road map' for the way ahead.

Engagement Skills Training (FATS)- begins realistic judgment-based training, focusing on themes presented in the legal presentation.

Weapon Manipulation- dry fire and live fire. Ensures that students have the requisite skills to safely and proficiently operate their weapons systems in close quarters shooting scenarios and during range based live fire judgment shooting drills. As the main mechanism that Soldiers employ when using deadly force, ensures that Soldiers are able to successfully use the weapon as a platform for range based live fire judgment shooting drills and scenario-based force on force Simunitions training.

Simulated Scenarios- judgment based training geared at accomplishing the themes outlined in the legal lecture. Training when to engage deadly force, and how to articulate actions after the fact.

OUTLINE OF INSTRUCTION
I. INTRODUCTION
One of the greatest trusts placed upon member of the Armed Forces is the responsibility of responding appropriately to a hostile act or demonstration of hostile intent. Part of this responsibility is to understand the Rules of Engagement and Rules for the Use of Force, and possess good judgment skills in applying use of force in self-defense. This requires assessing the facts and circumstances at the moment they are presented, and make a reasonable determination regarding an appropriate response.

This responsibility means that military personnel will be accountable for use of deadly force. The overall purpose of this course is to provide military personnel with a better understanding of the legal and tactical requirements in the use of force. Soldiers need to be proficient in knowing when not to use force, as well as be effective in employing force when necessary. They also need to fully understand it is acceptable to do so when confronted with an imminent threat of death or serious bodily injury, and that neither the law nor the rules require them to gamble with their lives.

II. LESSON PLAN PRESENTATION
Given a live scenario, the student will demonstrate the ability to make a rapid and legally correct use of force judgment and, if appropriate, engage in the timely and effective use of deadly force. The student will then demonstrate the ability to describe the reasons behind the decision that was made and defend his actions.

Each element of the course presentation must reflect a reiteration of the legal lecture on Day 1 and emphasize the purpose/objectives of the course as outlined above. The course is not designed to create a tactical operator or master weapon operator. The course is designed to expose Soldiers to judgment-based training to aid in the decision making process of when it is appropriate to use deadly force to stop a threat. The course is also aimed at providing a Soldier the tools necessary to articulate to a supervisor or investigator what actions the subject displayed that lead the Soldier to his objectively reasonable conclusion that deadly force was an appropriate response to deal with the threat presented.

III. LEGAL LECTURE

Throughout the lecture the student will gain insight and understanding in four main concepts or principles. These principles help develop the ability to make "objectively reasonable" decisions in deciding when to use deadly force to stop a threat. The four concepts are:

RULES OF FORCE- Mission-dependent, but will always provide a solid overview of the inherent right of self-defense and the objectivelly reasonable legal standard for using force in self-defense.

THREAT ASSESSMENT- Prior to using deadly force Soldiers must be able to identify that the subject of such force is a threat. As the enemy does not wear Al Qaeda t-shirts, threat assessment must be based on pre-assaultive indicators. In this manner, threat assessment mirrors law enforcement in that Soldiers often must act responsively to the actions of another, rather than proactively in eliminating a threat. Threat identification is based on three factors, and developed through examining patterns of learned behaviors:

Intent- the subject must demonstrate pre-assaultive behavior that would lead an objectively reasonable person to believe that the subject intended to inflict serious bodily injury or death.

Ability- the subject must demonstrate physical action that would lead an objectively reasonable person to believe that they had the means or ability to cause you serious bodily injury or death. This may be through the display of a weapon, but it may not be.

Opportunity- The suject must have the opportunity to cause you serious bodily injury or death. For example, if the subject is 15 feet away from you with a knife in his hand, he has the opportunity to do you harm. He will be able to get to you and cause you harm before you will be able to draw your weapon and attempt to disable him. However, if there is a 12 foot chain link fence between you and the subject, his opportunity to cause you harm vanishes.

UNDERSTANDING THE LAW- All actions of search or seizure of persons by agents of the government must be reasonable. The test of reasonable is a common sense evaluation of what another "objectively reasonable" person would have done in the same circumstances.

While *objective reasonableness is not capable of precise definition or mechanical application,* (Graham v. Connor) objective reasonableness will be determined as of the instant the force was used, rather than in the clear vision or 20-20 hindsight.

It will be determined by examining a number of factors that are involved in the Soldier's decision to use force. The reasonableness of the Soldier's decision will be based on the facts and circumstances known to the Soldier at the time force was used.

What was determined or discovered after force was used cannot be used to justify or condemn the use of force and would normally not be admissible evidence in a criminal proceeding.

The standard of objectively reasonable set forth in the Fourth Amendment does not require that Soldiers choose the least intrusive level of force, only a reasonable one.

If the use of deadly force is justified, the implement used to apply that force is of no consequence.

UNDERSTANDING THE DYNAMICS OF AN ENCOUNTER
Action v. Reaction.
Tache-Psyche Effect.
Wounds Ballistics.

OODA/PADE- There are several different "cycles" of steps in deciding what to do when faced with a confrontation that may necessitate deadly force.

OODA. Developed by Air Force fighter pilot Colonel John Boyd. Under Boyd's cycle prior to acting in response to a stimulus, one must:
Observe the stimulus. You can't respond to what you don't know about

(situational awareness is key here). Then you must **Orient** yourself to the stimulus and **Decide** upon an appropriate action given the stimulus presented. Finally you **Act** upon the stimulus in carrying out your decision.

"Orientation shapes observation, shapes decision, shapes action, and in turn, is shaped by the feedback and other phenomena coming into our sensing or observing window…the entire "loop" (not just orientation) is an ongoing many-sided implicit cross-referencing process of projection, empathy, correlation, and rejection."—Colonel John Boyd.

PADE. Under this condition cycle, one must **Perceive** a danger or threat. You must know what danger is specifically- it is a specific threat to yourself or another. Upon perceiving a danger or threat, you must **Analyze** the stimulus and determine if it is directed at you or not. Discriminate acts of violence to remove self doubt and hesitation. You then **Decide** on a response. Minimize your options for what your decision will be (Hick's Law). The fewer options you have, the faster you'll be in making your decision and transitioning to the final stage of the cycle, **Execution**.

Once you understand the steps involved in responding to a subject's actions, you need to know how to speed your response time up, while slowing/disaffecting their reaction time. By the time you enter the equation the bad guy is likely already in decision, if not act/execute. There is no means of catching up without forcing the bad guy out of his place in the cycle, or re-setting his clock. You do this through Surprise, Aggression, and Speed. The three cornerstones of CQB as recognized in the Army are Surprise, Speed and Violence of Action.

IV. ENGAGEMENT SKILLS TRAINING (EST) or FIREARMS TRAINING SYSTEM (FATS)

Soldiers will be presented with computer-driven simulated scenarios and asked to respond accordingly. Upon completion of each exercise the soldier will be "debriefed" and asked to articulate the reasons for actions taken. Non-participating Soldiers will observe the scenario and upon completion of the exercise will be separated from the participating soldier and asked to articulate their observations. The observers and the actor will then be brought together and asked to give their statement of what they did/observed. Differences will be highlighted, and emphasized that both may be justifiable, even if different, as long as each are objectively reasonable given the situation presented in the scenario.

Scenario Development: Law Enforcement and Military scenarios will be used in connection with EST/FATS training. Alternate shoot/noshoot scenarios, and escalate/de-escalate scenarios, too, sometimes based on student's command voice and ability to gain dominance tactically. An EST session for 25 soldiers will require approximately 2.5 hours of instruction. Every student should go through at least one scenario. Students not participating in a scenario should be required to observe because they can learn by watching. Observers will receive the same instruction through observation and participation in the after action debriefing. Each scenario should take approximately 2-10 minutes to complete, and 10-15 minutes to debrief.

V. WEAPON SKILLS

The focus of the weapons section of the course is to provide Soldiers with basic weapons safety and operation skills to better prepare them for the simulated scenarios that encompass the final two days of training. The focus of the course is to guide Soldiers in making decisions regarding the use of deadly force, which is best accomplished through judgment based, reality intensive training. However, to successfully teach judgement decisions regarding the application of deadly force, Soldiers' focus must be on the threat and responding to the threat, and should not be hindered by their inability to operate their weapon system quickly, efficiently, and safely. Soldiers must be able to safely operate their weapon system, keep the weapon running, and accurately place shots on the intended target. Operating the weapon system should eventually become second nature, leaving the soldier better able to allocate mental resources on the threat(s) and to make appropriate decisions regarding elimination of said threat(s). Remember: basic weapon operation and remediation. No high speed drills that will overwhelm students and compromise the effectiveness of the live fire portion of the course.

Instructors must present a unified platform for weapon operation. Recognizing that there is more than one "correct" way to perform many of the below listed skills, the following are the methods taught in this

ROE/RUF course. **Given appropriate time, Instructors should teach the skill and the <u>reasoning</u> behind the skill.** It is not enough to know how to do something- Soldiers must be given the "why" behind the skill. This is critical for non-standard situations where the skill taught may not be appropriate for situation the soldier faces. If the soldier does not understand why we taught a particular method, the soldier will not understand when that method may not be appropriate, and change the tactic accordingly.

Soldiers will be presented with two blocks of instruction regarding operation of both the M9 pistol and M4 carbine consisting of a block of dry-fire instruction and a block of live fire instruction. Instruction must be kept to basic skills and safety lessons as Soldiers are provided limited hours of instruction. Soldiers will not become expert marksmen or operators on either weapon in the time allotted, and exposure to too many skill sets will frustrate and impede the learning process. It is better to settle on a few very important skill sets and accomplish those, than to expose students to too much and risk overload and shut down. The methods taught must be simple, have multiple applications, and promote economy of motion.

The following are the skills necessary to convey in order to accomplish the course mission and safely and effectively conduct the final two days of scenario-based simunition training:

    Safety
    Proper Body Stance / Position
    Presentation of the Weapon
    Drawing the Pistol from a Ready Position or Holster
    Mounting the Carbine from a Ready Position
    Firing Sequence
    Aiming the Weapon at an Intended Target
    Trigger Control
    Recovery from Each Shot / Recovery and Follow Through
    Manipulations
    Loading the Weapon
    Unloading the Weapon
    Reloading the Weapon
    Immediate Action
    Remedial Action

The skills listed above will be taught through dry and live fire drills and sequences. These drills should attempt to incorporate as much of the principles of the legal lecture as possible, but be flexible for time, ammunition supply, and skill level of the Soldiers participating in training. At the end of each weapon system lesson plan is a chart of the course of fire for presenting these skill sets. The courses of fire are designed to take less than the time allocated, leaving flex time for each weapon system. Instructors must keep track of time to ensure completion of all drills within the allocated time. The flex time should be used to tailor instruction for the particular group of students based on their skill level. If additional time is needed on a particular drill, the schedule must be flexible enough to provide the needed instruction. However, if the course of fire is completed with time to spare, additional drills are included following the core curriculum. No new skills should be taught in these additional drills. They are designed to re-emphasize the skills taught during the standard course of fire, but do so in a different manner, namely through fun exercises or minimal competition. Competition can be a positive teaching tool, but must be tailored to the skill set of the students. Competitions should show Soldiers their weaknesses and areas for improvement, but also show their improvements / accomplishments. Students should leave the range feeling positive about their accomplishments that day; not necessarily feeling that they possess perfect skills (there is always room for improvement) but that they have dramatically improved their weapon operation skills, were exposed to a solid base of skills to expand upon, and that they do possess the skills necessary to survive a deadly force encounter if necessary.

RULES FOR SAFE WEAPON HANDLING

Instructor Note: Stop and Explain Each Rule, Don't Breeze Through Them! Give Real World Examples Of Where Failure to Follow the Rule Resulted in Good Guy Injury.

1) Treat all guns as if they are always loaded.
2) Do not point the muzzle at anything you do not want to destroy- this includes your own body parts.
3) Keep you finger off the trigger until the sights of your weapon are on the intended target.

4) **Know your target and what lies beyond.**

PISTOL

It is the consensus of most tactical firearms instructors that if one can master the pistol, then good carbine shooting follows. In other words, mastery of a pistol—with a much shorter sight radius—is more difficult than mastery of a carbine. That is why the MTT generally spends more time with this weapon system.

Dry Fire Drills: Safe Weapon Manipulation

A. Safety—Two rules:

    a. **1st Rule of Weapon Safety—Muzzle Control**
      - don't point weapon at anything you don't want to kill/destroy
      - whose responsibility—shooter

    b. **2nd Rule of Weapon Safety—Index Trigger Finger**
      - finger off trigger until weapon on target and you're ready to shoot
      - where to put it?—we call that "indexing" your trigger finger, fingers straight, along slide or frame above trigger guard

B. Weapon Familiarization—M9 (Beretta 92FS 9mm)

    a. **TDA weapon**—traditional double action, 1st shot double action, second shot single action (explain what happens, discuss heavy 1st round DA trigger pull, much lighter follow-up SA shots)

    b. **Controls**
      - Decocker/Safety—does two things:
      - press down decocks, puts on safe
      - press back up, puts on fire
      - NEVER decock by using thumb on hammer
      - Slide Lock—Locks slide to rear, releases to load round
      - Take Down Lever

    c. **Load, Unload and Lock Open**
      - Magazine Release/Magazine Well/Magazine

C. Equipment Placement

a. Two goals
- easy access
- secure

b. Specifics
- thigh holster (Safariland, placement)
- holster on MOLLE gear/body armor (Blackhawk CQC Serpa)
- magazine pouches (belt, top row of MOLLE straps on body armor)
- eye/ear protection

D. Stance

a. "Fighting stance"
- like natural boxing stance
- mobility; good lateral movement: L-R, F-B
- 360° Scan Ability—why do we scan?
- demonstrate

Instructors Note: Demonstrate ability to move forward, sideways, and backwards using both this position, and the traditional more bladed Weaver-style position.

Demonstrate areas of vulnerability for Weaver-style bladed position (gap in body armor under arm- don't want that area as part of your body immediately facing downrange)

Another rationale that mitigates against Weaver and in favor of Isoceles is that it works in concert with rather than against the natural reactions of the human body. In a fight people square off and unless they are punching they will push off against the opponent w/ both hands. The Isoceles stance reflects what the human body does under stress, pushing forward with both hands, while Weaver does not.

Demonstrate stability of the platform. Have a student stand in traditional bladed Weaver-style position with arms extended as if they were presenting a pistol on a target. Stand in front of them and push back on their extended arms. They likely will take a step backwards. Do the same after having the student stand in the Universal Fighting Stance. If positioned properly, the student should absorb the push and not move.

E. Grip

a. Thumbs Point Forward
 - place on frame or slide
 - good place for support hand thumb is take down lever
 - won't hurt shooter's hand/fingers or effect function of weapon

b. Lock Wrists at 45°

c. Isolate movement of Trigger Finger
 - avoid tendency to "milk" grip when pressing trigger

d. Palms Together—Surround Stock
 - wrap around grip
 - support hand at 45° angle, fill in empty space on grip

F. Draw

a. Four-Five part action: Move quickly but in control (Slow is Smooth; Smooth is Fast—Economy of Motion—draw fast, shoot slow)
 - Grip
 - Rip/Pop/Clear
 - Rotate—barrel parallel to ground, pointed towards threat/target
 - Transition—hands move together on grip (natural hand-clap position, middle of chest/body)
 - Extension (High Ready)—arms extended, sights on target (Isosceles)
   - stance—create supporting triangle w/
   - arms/shoulders, not Weaver or modified
   - Weaver—discuss differences here)

b. Work trigger as gun is pressed out and into line of sight from Transition to Full Extension (High Ready)

c. Scan in High Ready position (Extension) on target—Why? don't get fixated on any one point, retain situational awareness

d. After engagement—Re-holster—reverse of draw:
 - Bring weapon back into the transition position
 - Finger off trigger—"Index"
 - Continue scan

- De-cock weapon = de-cock, place back on fire (demonstrate support hand sweep method of de-cocking and placing back on fire)
- Re-holster—dominant hand only, support hand stays in center of chest

G. Sight Alignment

a. **Equal light on both sides of the front sight post (explain)**
b. **Equal height—front and rear sights are same height across the top**
c. **Focus on Front Sight only—we say "front sight clear."**
   - human eye can only focus on one object at a time, the rest are in the peripheral vision, you're aware of it but not focused on it
d. **Place front sight post just below point of aim/point of impact (target)**

H. Trigger Press

a. **Press with first joint of index finger**
b. **Finger off trigger when sights off target**
c. **Reset for follow up shots—Two methods (explain and demonstrate both):**
   - short reset—finger stays on trigger, reset stroke is short
   - flip and press—finger off trigger, long reset stroke (index finger might actually hit front of trigger guard)

I. Magazine Changes

a. **Two Types: Slide Lock Reload & Tactical Reload—natural hand clap position**
b. **<u>Slide Lock Reload</u>—gun is empty, slide locked to rear**
   - <u>Access spare magazine</u>
   - mags w/ rounds facing forward/center of body (either in pouches on side opposite holster or on upper chest mounted on MOLLE gear/body armor)
   - index finger of support hand near top of mag, near front of top round, use as guide to access magazine well
   - <u>Drop empty magazine</u>—concurrent w/ accessing spare using

shooting hand thumb (or support hand sweep method for
those w/ smaller hands)
- Insert fresh magazine—use heel of support hand, slam it in good
- Activate slide release (or rack slide–slingshot or over the top—know
and explain relative advantages/disadvantages of both w/ the M9)

c. Tactical Reload—pause in fight, running low but not empty,
need to reload
- Remove old magazine—shooting hand thumb or support
hand sweep
- place in pocket or dump pouch
- Access spare magazine—mags w/rounds facing forward/center
of body (either in pouches on side opposite holster or on upper
chest mounted on MOLLE gear/body armor)
- index finger of support hand near top of mag, near front of top
round, use as guide to access magazine well
- Insert fresh magazine—use heel of support hand, slam it in good
- Activate slide release (or rack slide–slingshot or over the top—
know and explain relative advantages/disadvantages of both
w/ the M9)

J. Immediate Action Drills (IAD)—three basic malfunctions:

a. Failure to Fire
- Tap-Rack-Ready/Bang
c. Failure to Eject ('Stove Pipe')
- Sweep with support hand
e. Everything Else
- Lock-Rip-Work-Tap-Rack-Bang/Ready

K. Range Commands

a. "De-cock"—de-cock weapon and put back on fire (de-cocking lever up)
b. "De-cock on safe"—de-cock weapon and leave on safe (de-cocking lever down)
c. "Re-holster"—de-cock weapon, place back on fire, and put in holster

- NEVER re-holster a weapon that has the hammer cocked
- unless told otherwise always re-holster w/weapon de-cocked and set on fire

d. "Load your weapons"—magazine in weapon, round loaded in chamber, weapon
   de-cocked, weapon in holster or drill start position as directed by instructor

e. "Clear your weapons"
   - drop magazine
   - clear weapon by racking slide 3 times
   - lock slide to rear
   - observe chamber and magazine well to ensure there is no round in chamber and no magazine in magazine well
   - show to coach who should make same observations
   - activate slide lock to drop slide forward
   - dry fire once downrange by pulling trigger and allowing hammer to fall on empty chamber
   - place weapon on safe
   - re-holster

Basic Handgun Class: 300 Rounds
(Approx. 15 mags @ 15 rds ea.; 6 mags @ 10 rds ea.; 2 mags @ 2 rds ea. w/ 10 loose rounds; 1 mag @ 15 rds + 1 in chamber)

Drill #	Ammo Count	Concept	Notes	Target	Distance
1	1 mag/10 rnds (10)	1 hole drill	Single shots; high ready - own pace (slow); fundamentals	3" Dot	7 yards
1a	1 mag/10 rnds (20)	1 hole drill	Single shots; low ready - own pace (slow); fundamentals	3" Dot	7 yards
1b	1 mag/10 rnds (30)	1 hole drill	Single shots; transition - own pace (slow); fundamentals	3" Dot	7 yards
2	1 mag/15 rnds (45)	Multiple Shots	Multiple shots (2-4); high ready - on command	8" plate	7 yards
2a	1 mag/15 rnds (60)	Multiple Shots	Multiple shots (2-4); low ready - on command	8" plate	7 yards
2b	1 mag/15 rnds (75)	Multiple Shots	Multiple shots (2-4); transition - on command	8" plate	7 yards
3	1 mag/10 rnds (85)	1 hole drill from the draw; develop "hard-wire"	Single shots; draw (DHP) - own pace (slow)	3" Dot	7 yards
4	1 mag/15 rnds (100)	Single shots from draw	Single shots; draw (DHP); - on command	8" plate	7/10 yards
5	2 mags/30 rnds (130)	Multiple Shots from draw	Multiple shots (2-4); draw (DHP) - on command	8" plate	7/10 yards
6	2 mags/14 rds (load ea. mag w/ 2 rds); rest of rds in pocket (144)	Mag changes; slide-lock and tactical reload (from cover)	Multiple shots (1-4) - two double taps/ Mozambique; draw (DHP) - on command; [concept: two, slide-lock reload, two (2x); two, tac reload, one (2x)]	8" plate	7 yards

Drill #	Ammo Count	Concept	Notes	Target	Distance
1	1 mag/10 rnds (10)	1 hole drill	Single shots; high ready - own pace (slow); fundamentals	3" Dot	7 yards
1a	1 mag/10 rnds (20)	1 hole drill	Single shots; low ready - own pace (slow); fundamentals	3" Dot	7 yards
1b	1 mag/10 rnds (30)	1 hole drill	Single shots; transition - own pace (slow); fundamentals	3" Dot	7 yards
2	1 mag/15 rnds (45)	Multiple Shots	Multiple shots (2-4); high ready - on command	8" plate	7 yards
2a	1 mag/15 rnds (60)	Multiple Shots	Multiple shots (2-4); low ready - on command	8" plate	7 yards
2b	1 mag/15 rnds (75)	Multiple Shots	Multiple shots (2-4); transition - on command	8" plate	7 yards
3	1 mag/10 rnds (85)	1 hole drill from the draw; develop "hard-wire"	Single shots; draw (DHP) - own pace (slow)	3" Dot	7 yards
4	1 mag/15 rnds (100)	Single shots from draw	Single shots; draw (DHP); - on command	8" plate	7/10 yards
5	2 mags/30 rnds (130)	Multiple Shots from draw	Multiple shots (2-4); draw (DHP) - on command	8" plate	7/10 yards
6	2 mags/14 rds (load ea. mag w/ 2 rds); rest of rds in pocket (144)	Mag changes; slide-lock and tactical reload (from cover)	Multiple shots (1-4) - two double taps/ Mozambique; draw (DHP) - on command; [concept: two, slide-lock reload, two (2x); two, tac reload, one (2x)]	8" plate	7 yards

DHP—Dedicated Hand Position UCP—Universal Cover Position

- high guard
- surrender
- at sides
- natural hand-clap (waist)
- holding object
- behind back

weapon at full extension, aimed at threat/subject belt line.

Low Ready—45° angle @ base of target

High Ready—aimed @ target, finger indexed

Transition—pistol in middle of chest, parallel to ground, held in both hands

2 Hr. Basic Pistol DV Compressed Class: 105 Rounds
(5 mags @ 15 rds ea.; 3 mags @ 10 rds ea.)

Drill #	Ammo Count	Concept	Notes	Target	Distance
1	1 mag/10 rnds (10)	One hole drill	Single shots; transition – own pace (slow); fundamentals	3" Dot	7 yards
2	1 mags/15 rnds (25)	Multiple Shots	Multiple shots (2-4); transition - on command	8" plate	7 yards
3	1 mag/10 rnds (35)	Single shots from draw	Single shots; draw (DHP); - on command	8" plate	7 yards
4	1 mag/15 rnds (50)	Multiple shots from draw	Multiple shots (2-4); draw (DHP); - on command	8" plate	7 yards
5	1 mag/15 rnds (65)	Move off-line from attack (1 step Left or Right)	Multiple shots (2-3); draw (DHP); - on command	8" plate	7 yards
6	2 mags/30 rnds (95)	Shoot-No-Shoot judgment drills – "decision making overload"	Decision making drills; colors, shapes, numbers, letters; (add 1 step L-R on last mag); Multiple shots (1-4); draw (DHP) – on command	Cardboard, IDPA or paper – colors/ numbers/shapes/ letters	7 yards
7	1 mag/10 rnds (105)	Man-on-Man	Test/Competition; 1" round – double elim.; 2nd round – single elim.; Single/Multiple shots; draw (DHP) – on command	Pepper poppers	7 yards

DHP—Dedicated Hand Position UCP—Universal Cover Position

- high guard   weapon at full extension, aimed at
- surrender   threat/subject belt line
- at sides   Low Ready—45° angle @ base of target
- natural hand-clap (waist) High Ready—aimed @ target, finger indexed
- holding object   Transition—pistol in middle of chest, parallel
- behind back   to ground, held in both hands

Additional Drill if Time Permits

Ask Soldiers what skills they would like to work on, or permit recreational fire (Soldiers can practice what they want, or at least get additional trigger time). In some cases Soldiers may not want to speak up to the group, and may ask individual instructors that they've been working with to help them during "recreational fire." Instructors should discretely signal the rangemaster and see if class as whole wants to work on the drill the soldier brought to the instructor's attention. If one wants additional practice on that skill, there's probably another that does, too.

CARBINE

DRY FIRE

During the 2-hour block of dry fire instruction, students should be taught all the basic skills listed above. For purposes of this course, the following techniques/methods will be used for carbine instruction.

There are no "do-overs." If a student "messes up" on any portion of the instruction, the instructors must encouage them to continue through with the drill and follow through on all actions. They will then be given a second opportunity to complete the exercise without the "mess up."

Complete Dry Fire with unloaded and confirmed clear weapons and no ammunition in the same area. Visually and tactiley inspect the weapon and confirm with the next shooter on the line.

Proper Body Stance / Position
Presentation of the Weapon
    Mounting the Carbine from a Ready Position
Firing Sequence
    Aiming the Weapon at an Intended Target
    Trigger Control
    Recovery from Each Shot / Recovery and Follow Through
Manipulations
    Loading the Weapon
    Unloading the Weapon
    Reloading the Weapon
    Immediate Action
    Remedial Action
    Transition to Pistol (time permitting)

LIVE FIRE

Recognize when to pull a student off line if not up to skill level necessary to safely perform live fire drills. Only Teach One Skill At a Time. Start Slow, Build Up. Add new skills building on previous skills.

Low Ready

Learn Basics—Stance, snap up and in, Grip, Sight Picture, Trigger Control. Marksmanship Drills.

Use 6" target so students can get hits.

Start with slow fire, move to multiple shots with trigger reset, and then NSR.

Decrease Size of Target—start with slow fire, move to multiple shots, add decision making- 6 pack target

Add Distance—start with slow fire on 6-pack target, move to 2 shots on draw.

Add Manipulations- go back to closer distances.

Speed Reload, Tactical Reload, Immediate Action Drill

Add Movement

Pivot Drills- left, right, 6:00-right, 6:00-left (and reasoning, i.e.,bulkhead) "Weave" drill- (perform dry)

Movement forward (with instructor holding shirt/belt)

Movement rearward

Lateral Movement

Specific Simulation Drills

Bomb Drill-(head shot) with time stress- this is a smaller target, so go back in on distances first.

Multiple Areas- transitioning between areas on the target.

Pull It All Together

Color Targets at Distance- have 4 colors on a target, one color was identified as your "good guy" color. Don't remind them. Look for both decision making, and sympathetic firing- if they hear others shoot, will they? Even if it's the wrong color? Think about what you're simulating- someone fires at something, everyone needs to do their own assessment before firing.

Culmination—Elimination Drill. Set it up so that everyone can advance, and don't make it unrealistic. "Competition" must still convey a lesson.

Carbine Course of Fire

Yard	Drill	Rounds	Skill Conveyed
15	5&1 cm,(5 times)	5	Weapon Presentation
15	2 magazines, 1 round in each 1 cm, IAD, 1 cm(5 times)	10	Immediate Action Drill
15	5&1 cm, pivot to the right (5 times) *Colors Called*	5	Right Turn
15	5&1 cm, pivot to the left (5 times)	5	Left Turn
15	5&1 cm, 180° to the right (5 times)	5	180° Turn to the Right
15	5&1 cm, 180° to the left (5 times)	5	180° Turn to the Left

All stages begin from the low ready

END First 2 Hour Segment
BEGIN 4 Hour Segment

Yard	Drill	Rounds	Skill Conveyed
15	1 shot drills (5 times)	5	Dot Torture (6-pack target; each target has 6 3 inch numbered circles). Instructor calls numbers.
10	1 shot drills (5 times)	5	
7	1 shot drills (5 times)	5	
7	Advance. Fire between 2-5 rounds (NSR) center mass, between 15-7 yard line. (remediate weapon as needed) *repeat between 10-15 times*	50	Shooting on the Move
15	Engage front target (NSR-CM), Engage one of side targets with 1 head shot. *Repeat between 3-5 times*	15	Multiple target engagement
15	Color called, NSR *(repeat between 8-13 times)*	35	Decision Making. Instructor calls colors. (1 color is always a no-shoot)

From here on, place 4 color pages on each target. One color designated permanent no-shoot. Instructor calls color(s) prior to each drill.

Yard	Drill	Rounds	Skill Conveyed
25	2 cm, 3.0 seconds	2	Shooters with positive hits within time move to 20
20	1 cm, 1 head shot, 4.5 seconds	2	Shooters with positive hits within time move to 15
15	1 cm, reload, 1 cm, 6.0 seconds	2	Shooters with positive hits within time move to 7
7	Empty chamber, loaded mag. 1 head shot (shooters must sight weapon and attempt to fire before charging weapon), 4.5 seconds	1	Shooters with positive hits within time move to 5
5	1 head shot, 1.5 seconds	1	

Elimination Drill- 1 color page pasted center mass, ¼ at head. Total Drill Performed 2x

160 rounds per student

VI. NLTA SCENARIOS—MOUT (MILITARY OPERATIONS IN URBAN TERRAIN)

This portion of the lesson plan was developed to assist the trainer with the design and implementation of firearms training using Non-Lethal Training Ammunition (NLTA). A multi-person team is tasked with the development and implementation of a variety of training exercises using the SIMUNITION FX marking cartridge or other NLTA. Before every iteration, the trainers will review safety issues, scenario development, logistical support, planning, design and the proper execution of interactive training using NLTA technology.

ENABLING PERFORMANCE OBJECTIVES (EPO):

EPO #1: Discuss Survival stress, mental preparation and crisis rehearsals.

EPO #2: Discuss the "Phases of Training Concept" and how NLTA can supplement traditional firearms training.

EPO #3: Discuss the weapons, ammunition, protective equipment, facilities, and personnel needed to safely conduct interactive training using NLTA.

EPO #4: Discuss the elements of scenario development and other NLTA applications

EPO #5: Discuss role player guidelines.

EPO #6: Demonstrate interactive training by participating as a team member during a variety of group exercises using NLTA.

TRAINING AIDS/EQUIPMENT:

Instructor:

Knowledge of interactive training goals and objectives.

Knowledge of the ROE/RUF Tactical Training Seminar SOP regarding NLTA

Trauma kit

Various items to be used as cover/concealment, e.g., vehicle, mailbox, barrels, fire hydrant, trees, structures etc.

Additional props as necessary, e.g., AOR-specific clothing, dress or uniforms, radios, and rubber knives/weapons.

Appropriate weapons, ammunition, and protective equipment.

Controllable training area

Safety officer/facilitator

Ensure that all weapons used are designated for interactive training applications (Color code-BLUE), and have proper conversion kits installed to permit live target engagement (but NOT the chambering of live rounds).

Ensure that all ammunition used is approved NLTA, e.g., SIMUNITION FX cartridge or paintball.

Student:

Knowledge of interactive training goals and objectives.

Knowledge of the Safety SOP (via briefing) regarding NLTA.

Appropriate training weapon, ammunition, and protective equipment Weapon(s) converted for interactive applications (Color code-BLUE) to permit live target engagement.

Appropriate NLTA

NLTA protective equipment.

INSTRUCTOR SPECIAL REQUIREMENTS:

Instructors must verify that all weapons and ammunition are designated for NLTA applications and live target engagements

Compliance with the SOP regarding NLTA.

Instructors should supervise the loading of all magazines.

INTRODUCTION:

In most schools (especially military ones) the traditional tool used for teaching and measuring firearm proficiency is the Qualification Course. While there is no debate that the shooting skills developed and reinforced during Qualification—the ability to accurately engage targets to a known distance—are important, trainers must also recognize the limitations inherent with this style of "Static" firearms training. Over the years, leading training authorities (civilian & military) have also acknowledged that static target shooting alone is not enough to effectively prepare individuals for the types of conditions often experienced when firearms are used in the field. The use of NLTA in a training program allows for situational exercises and training opportunities that transcend traditional firearms training. This lesson plan will provide the trainer with essential information regarding the safe and effective use of NLTA as part of a "holistic" training program.

LESSON PLAN OVERVIEW:

Terminal performance objective (TPO)

Given appropriate weapons converted to fire NLTA, protective equipment and logistical support, the trainer will actively participate as a team member tasked with the development and execution of interactive training exercises using the SIMUNITION FX marking cartridge or other NLTA.

EPO #1: Discuss Survival stress, mental preparation and crisis rehearsals.

During a high stress incident, individuals will experience physiological changes caused by the involuntary/automatic activation of the sympathetic nervous system (SNS). The SNS is activated anytime the brain perceives an event as extremely dangerous or potentially life threatening. The result is an immediate discharge of stress hormones, (often referred to as an "adrenaline dump"), into the bloodstream as the body prepares for what is recognized as the "Fight, Flight or Freeze response."

These changes are the body's normal reactions to abnormal conditions and they will affect performance to some extent. Once understood, individuals can better learn to manage themselves and to counter and/or minimize the negative effects of the event. Advantages include additional strength, acute awareness and an increased pain threshold. The disadvantages include:

Increased heart rate and respiration.

General muscle tightening/shakes. Caused by the sudden mixing of epinephrine and sodium in muscle groups. When combined with the vascular flow away from the extremities and increased heart rate etc., the individual's ability to perform complex and fine motor skills will noticeably decrease and a loss of dexterity will be experienced.

Tunnel vision—also known as perceptual narrowing—occurs when the threatened individual loses most of their peripheral vision.

Auditory exclusion/Tunnel hearing. This is when sounds such as gunfire, people yelling or screaming etc., are not heard or sound muffled and distant.

Visual slowdown or time spatial distortion. The threatened individual may experience events in slow motion or lose track of normal periods.

Mental Preparation:

"Mindset" is a term used to describe an individual's state of mental readiness to act or react to stimulus in one's environment. "Mindset" should begin with the realization that all service members—regardless of their specialty—must be mentally prepared to use force when performing their official duties. More importantly, they should also realize that force might be directed at them because they are performing their official duties. A situation may be a low-level incident requiring a soft hands-on technique to gain compliance, a violent encounter with deadly consequences, or anywhere in between. In all cases, an accurate threat assessment and a decisive response are crucial for maintaining control and minimizing potential injury to all parties involved.

CRISIS REHEARSALS:

This is when students mentally prepare themselves beforehand, for potential crisis situations they may face on the job. It is accomplished by mentally rehearsing or visualizing a situation, placing yourself in that situation, and considering how you might handle it. Crisis rehearsals and visualization techniques build confidence and reduce response times because they act as mental triggers initiating a plan of action thought about in advance. Rather than thinking "Oh my god, I'm in a fight," the response should be "Here it is and I'm ready for" it. Important areas to consider are:

"Use of Force" policy- do you fully understand the authorities your have pursuant to the ROE/RUF? Is it clear in your mind when you could lawfully use your weapon or lesser means of force?

The "negotiate mentality"- some students are hesitant to use force even when their lives or the lives of others are in imminent danger of serious physical injury or death. There may be many reasons for this, but suffice it to say that there are times when verbal judo is applicable, and times when it is not.

Setting the mental trigger- this primarily refers to non-spontaneous events when the individual is ready but has not yet decided to apply force. It is a means of establishing mental boundaries and deciding in advance, what movements or actions will trigger the application of force. For example, you are covering a suspect with a gun visible in his waistband. You are using verbal commands to keep his hands away from the gun. You are not shooting yet because he appears to be complying and you don't yet feel imminent danger. Your mental trigger should be "if he reaches for the gun I'm going to shoot until the threat is stopped." Mental triggers may be any number of things but they must always be sufficient in the mind of the individual to justify their use of force.

Post incident—Many warriors, even if prepared mentally and physically to survive a violent confrontation, may not understand the myriad of emotional after-effects. Take the time to learn what they are and what to expect. Of great importance, however, leaders must insulate their troops from any attempt by law enforcement or other investigators to interrogate or take sworn statements from a Soldier at 0300 in a TOC.

EPO #2: Discuss the "Phases of Training Concept" and how NLTA can supplement traditional firearms training.
Most physical training can be classified into one of three phases or levels of training. These levels, Static, Dynamic, and Interactive are used to define training, evaluate training goals, and to improve individual performance. The system is designed to build upon learned skills and provide career long growth and development. The concept is similar to the crawl, walk, run adage because the process uses a progressive building block approach with training. By progressing through the levels, the student gains personal confidence and improves individual competence. More importantly, when participating in properly designed interactive exercises the student gains learned survival experiences via practical applications. Ultimately, the student is better prepared to

operate safely and effectively in the field. The phases of Training are:

Static Training- The student receives instruction about specific skills and techniques. Those skills and techniques are then practiced and developed via repetition in a static range or training environment. Primary emphasis is directed at isolating and enhancing the specific skills through repetition and drills.

Theories and techniques of survival shooting

Marksmanship fundamentals

PPC/Combat techniques

Static Reduced light

Basic shoulder fired weapons

Dynamic Training- Dynamic training provides a more realistic and challenging environment for the application and reinforcement of learned static skills. It introduces the fluid integration of decision making skills and tactical concerns, e.g., recognition and effective use of cover, shooter movement, engaging multiple or moving targets, and shoot/no-shoot judgments scenarios. Examples of Dynamic training include:

Video simulators

Steel/Stress type courses

Shooting and moving drills

Engaging multiple or moving targets

Primary to secondary weapon transition drills

Combined weapons courses

Team engagement drills

Interactive Training- Interactive training provides the most realistic degree of training because there is true interaction with people. When working with role players the student must continually assess the situation and the subjects' actions, responding with appropriate use of force. When combined with NLTA such as the SIMUNITION FX marking cartridge or paintballs, the stress levels and heart-rate are noticeably increased and job-related performance is more accurately evaluated. When problem areas are identified, corrective actions can be taken to improve performance and confidence by increasing the skill builders during the previous levels of training. Success at this level requires clearly identified objectives and tightly controlled scenarios. Examples of Interactive training:

Situation Awareness and Response

Interactive Cover Drills (Levels I & II)

Interactive Judgment Drills

Other exercises using human interaction and judgment skills

EPO #3: Discuss the weapons, ammunition, protective equipment, facilities, and personnel needed to safely conduct interactive training using NLTA.

WEAPONS:

NO LIVE WEAPONS, AMMUNITION, CHEMICAL IRRITANTS OR EDGED/IMPACT WEAPONS ARE PERMITTED IN THE TRAINING AREA. Only designated weapons properly converted to fire approved NLTA are permitted in the training environment. Under most circumstances, this means modifying the weapon to fire the SIMUNITION FX, marking cartridge but other designated training weapons may be used as well.

SIMUNITION- The Company "SIMUNITION" makes a variety of conversion kits for use with their FX marking cartridge. The kits are available for most weapon systems presently used in the military and law enforcement. Each kit comes with instructions for proper installation and once installed allows the weapon to function normally using the specialized ammunition. The conversion kits also reduce the likelihood of "live ammunition" being inadvertently chambered and fired. The conversion kits should not, however, be relied upon to prevent it. The conversion kits and installation procedures vary with the weapon system. Be sure to follow and save the instructions provided with the kit. Once a weapon is properly converted it should be clearly marked for easy recognition by students and staff. The ROE/RUF Tactical Training Seminar cadre uses color-coded and converted NLTA weapons. In addition, we recommend permanently converting and marking a block of weapons strictly for interactive applications using NLTA. It is our opinion that dedicated NLTA weapons increase our safety objectives. If however, weapons must be converted on-site, one designated NLTA instructor should be responsible for performing all the conversions and marking the weapons with BLUE tape. Common areas to mark include the grips, stock, fore end, slide and trigger guards.

PAINTBALL- standard recreational paintball rifles are often used for cover type courses. They use a CO2 propellant and fire a .68 caliber non-toxic paintball approximately 250 to 300 fps depending on the velocity adjustment. Impacts from this weapon are messy and more severe then with the SIMUNITION FX cartridge. They are not recommended for close quarter engagements.

OTHERS- other weapons may be approved by the on-site NLTA coordinator for specific applications but these must also be inspected and marked. Examples include, inert weapons used as props, or blank firing weapons used for sound effects. Blank firing weapons should not be used in close quarter engagements due to possible injury. Regardless of the weapon(s) used, all should be handled with the same degree of seriousness and responsibility afforded to "live" weapons. The four primary safety rules are:

Treat all firearms as if they were loaded! Make no exceptions.

Never point the muzzle at anything you do not intend to engage or intimidate.

The trigger finger should stay off the trigger until you are on target and the use of deadly force is imminent.

Be sure of your target and what is beyond.

AMMUNITION:

The two most common types of NLTA presently used are the SIMUNITION FX marking cartridge and standard recreational paintballs.

SIMUNITION FX MARKING CARTRIDGE. The Company "SIMUNITION" produces a variety of ammunition. The ONLY AMMUNITION SAFE TO USE FOR LIVE TARGET ENGAGEMENT IS THE "SIMUNITION FX MARKING CARTIDGE." The SIMUNITION FX marking cartridge is a reduced energy cartridge developed for live target engagements and is designed to cycle and function in a standard duty weapon after the appropriate conversion kit has been installed. The cartridge should not be reloaded and it should never be fired through unmodified weapons. The marking compound or "goop," is a non-toxic detergent based compound that is water-soluble for easy clean up. The most common colors are red and blue but others are available via contact with the company. When fired, the projectile travels approximately 400 fps and is capable of causing severe injury if misused. Safety equipment is mandatory and all training using the SIMUNITION system should be controlled and supervised.

PAINTBALLS- Standard recreational paintballs are inexpensive and come in a variety of colors. As mentioned earlier, they hit harder and are more difficult to clean when compared to the FX, but they are very useful for specific applications.

Mandatory Safety Equipment: (must be tested and approved). The safety equipment identified is designed to guard against NLTA impacts. It is not sufficient for full force contact exercises.

Students

Head gear/face mask able to defeat the SIMUNITION FX marking
    projectile (400 fps)

Throat guard

Chest protector or vest

Groin protection

Gloves

Protection for exposed skin, e.g., Raid jacket, flight suit, BDU's or
    similar outer garment.

Role Players: At a minimum, role players will wear the same safety equipment as the students. Additional equipment may be added as necessary to minimize bruising.

Safety/protective equipment selection criteria:

Does the safety equipment provide adequate coverage to prevent
    unnecessary injury to the wearer?

Does the safety equipment allow students to experience a pain penalty
    when hit, yet prevent injury?

Does the role player safety equipment protect against injury and guard
    against a pain penalty?

Does the equipment withstand the effects of the NLTA (does not
    puncture, crack, or become damaged when hit)?

Can the equipment be repeatedly cleaned and sanitized without damage?

Will the equipment work in the determined climate?

Are there a variety of sizes available?

Is the equipment cost effective?

Does the equipment allow the participants to perform the movements and actions required?

Does the headgear allow for communications and provide adequate ventilation to avoid fogging the face shield?

Does the eye wear/face shield meet established impact standards, i.e., ANZI, OSHA?

Does the equipment meet the established training goals and objectives?

Facilities: Almost any area can be effectively used with a minimum of preparation and site work. The site should, however, be somewhat isolated and/or have limited access for control and safety purposes. If using outdoors, team members should ensure site provided approximately 100 yards for stray projectiles. In some cases, it is also wise to notify the local authorities about the training in case they receive any calls about the activities. Once a site is selected, the exercise areas should be thoroughly examined for potential hazards. Look for anything that might pose a safety problem, e.g., breakable items, exposed nails, broken glass on the ground or other sharp objects, etc. Other areas to consider are:

Realistic setting if conducting scenarios

Controllable areas for security and staging

Site security/checkpoint to control access

Designated rooms, facilities and vehicles able to withstand the impact of marking cartridges. Paintballs will dent vehicle exteriors but the SIMU-NITION FX normally will not.

Personnel:

NLTA Coordinator: A designated NLTA coordinator must be present at any training session using NLTA. He/she will:

Oversee the training and insure all NLTA safety rules and procedures are followed and enforced.

Verify correct weapons and ammunition

Insure that personnel are assigned to the following areas:

Site security at the entry/exit point

Safety officer at the staging area

Facilitators/evaluators

Role players

Site Security: For safety reasons, there should always be a designated checkpoint to prevent unauthorized weapons, ammunition, people or other unwanted items from entering the training environment. Yellow police tape is useful for creating a physical barrier. An organized controlled checkpoint helps set the tone for the training and reduces the chance that prohibited items (live guns, ammunition, knives and chemical sprays etc.), will enter the training environment. Everyone must enter through the checkpoint where they are inspected for prohibited items. All available NLTA instructors should be present to assist with the initial clearing process. After that, one NLTA instructor is sufficient for stragglers and re-inspection.

Safety Officer: One NLTA instructor should be designated as the Safety Officer (SO). If weapons must be converted on-site, the SO will convert and mark the weapons at the entry/exit checkpoint. If vehicles will be used the SO must sterilize the interior area to prevent prohibited items. Once completed, the SO will respond to the staging area to conduct the final safety briefing.

Upon completion the SO will remain in the staging area to prep students, issue and receive weapons/`equipment and perform general oversight duties.

Evaluator/Facilitator: The evaluator/facilitator will receive the students from the safety officer, check them for proper safety equipment, provide any last minute information, then accompany them to their exercise. While at the exercise he/she will act as a safety monitor/facilitator and evaluator. Upon completion, he/she will accompany the student(s) back to the staging area.

EPO #4: Discuss the elements of scenario development and other NLTA applications.

10 steps for successful scenario development

> Teach from the simple to the complex. Start with basic scenarios/skills before moving to the complex.
>
> Determine objectives then design the training accordingly.
>
> Exercises should be as realistic as possible without sacrificing safety.
>
> Consider logistics and prop acquisition.
>
> Control the physical environment. Role-playing attracts an audience.

Avoid telling a student that he/she has been "killed" or ruled "dead.

Never make a scenario an "unwinnable" situation for student.

Train within organizational policy and make training relevant to the job.

Policy development/Scenario development committee

Trainers/subject matter experts

Commanders and other key leaders

Legal review. Other common examples of NLTA applications include but are not limited to: Interior and exterior force on force training scenarios, vehicle stop drills, building searches, room clearing drills, use of force evaluations/judgment drills, standing or downed disabled drills, movement drills, reaction drills, defensive tactics training, raid techniques and use of cover drills.

EPO #5: Discuss role player guidelines.

When performing scenarios, role players will either make or break the training event. After safety, role players are the most important component for successful training. Desirable role player traits include: tempered personality, ability to follow instructions and act according to role, willing to put forth an extra effort to provide consistent presentations. Additional guidelines: this is why its important that training cadre who understand all the nuances of the training program act as role players. This allows for the necessary flexibility to ad lib when appropriate.

Role players should rehearse to insure consistent presentation for each scenario.

Role players must have enough knowledge of the scenario to elicit the correct responses from the students.

Role players must not "ad lib" to the point of being counter productive.

Role players must adhere to the established scenario objectives when accurately fired upon and await the student to bring the situation to a satisfactory conclusion.

It is the role player's job to lose, but not to give up so easily as to instill a false sense of confidence or ability in a student. While the student should emerge from an encounter as a winner, the student(s) should only be allowed to win through the application of appropriate techniques.

Role players must follow all safety rules and procedures and be completely protected to receive a high volume of marking cartridges.

INSTRUCTION (dry)

Room Clearing

Keep this very simple. Some Soldiers will have had exposure, others will not. For groups where there are students who are experienced, run through it one time with them, and let them teach back to the students who are not as familiar with the techniques.

Types of Room Entry- center fed and corner fed

Pre-Entry

Stack/Security/Communication

Use of devices (flash bangs, frags, etc)

Entry

Button-Hook

Criss-Cross

Fatal funnel/Corners Get You Killed

Vehicle Check Points

Entry Control Points

CHECKLIST AND SAFETY BRIEF

NLTA CHECKLIST

Designate and maintain a controlled training environment by establishing a perimeter entry/exit checkpoint.

Conduct "Physical" inspections for "Live" weapons and ammunition before training begins. Inspections should be conducted in pairs i.e., "buddy check" and include the following:

Each person must inspect themselves and all of their equipment looking for "Live" weapons & ammunition, to include edged, impact and chemical. <u>Live Weapons and ammunition must be removed from the training environment. If items can not be removed they must be declared & turned over to the Safety Officer for security & safekeeping</u>. If vehicles and/or buildings/facilities are part of the exercise, they must be inspected as well.

Each person will conduct an inspection of their "buddy" and their associated equipment.

The Safety Officer(s) will then conduct a final inspection using a

physical pat and crush inspection. If available, use a hand held
metal detector.

Visually inspect the NLTA training weapons (color-coded blue) for
conversion kits and verify appropriate NLTA.

Instructors must prepare all magazines for the NLTA weapons. The students however should load and charge their NLTA weapons, on
instructor command, to verify and acknowledge the condition of
their weapon.

Familiarize the participants with the safety equipment & show them
how to wear it properly.

Conduct a final student safety briefing.

Insure that everyone observing, evaluating, or videotaping scenarios is
wearing the designated protective gear while training is in progress.

Assign adequate site security personnel, as needed, to prevent unauthorized entry into the controlled training environment.

Conduct debriefing immediately following training

NLTA SAFETY BRIEFING- The following safety rules must be
explained before each training session begins. Exceptions or modifications
to these rules are only permitted for those exercises where the written training objectives specifically identify modifications in the lesson plan utilized
for the training e.g., Fragment drills.

NO LIVE WEAPONS/AMMUNITION/CHEMICAL IRRITANTS
OR EDGED/IMPACT WEAPONS ARE PERMITTED IN THE
TRAINING AREA.

Treat the NLTA weapon with same degree of seriousness and responsibility afforded a "live" weapon & ammunition.

Do not load until directed to do so.

Indiscriminate firing, unsafe or frivolous behavior will not be tolerated.

All participants must wear designated safety equipment and the equipment must remain in place until an instructor ends the exercise e.g., "OUT
OF ROLE", "CEASE FIRE" or loud whistle blast.

Upon hearing "OUT OF ROLE," "CEASE FIRE" or a loud whistle
blast, stop all activity immediately.

If a helmet or throat guard becomes dislodged during exercises immediately protect yourself by covering the exposed area and begin shouting "CEASE FIRE" or "OUT OF ROLE."

No one will go for your gun; there are no tricks.

Do not physically fight with, punch, kick, strike or otherwise abuse the role players.

If deadly force becomes necessary follow agency policy, guidelines and training regarding the Use of Force

For safety purposes do not shoot closer then 5 feet.

Do not give up or quit until stopped by an instructor. Injury or unsafe situations are exceptions.

Report all injuries to the instructor, immediately.

SIMUNITION SCENARIOS

Scenarios, as enemy Tactics, Techniques and Procedures (TTPs) are limited only by the imgaination and physical constraints of a target or area. Below, however, are some samples that have been used by previous iterations of the ROE/RUF Tactical Training Seminar:

SIMUNITION SCENARIOS
CHECKPOINT-DISMOUNTED

Scenario 1

Shoot or No-Shoot: No shoot

Set-Up/Conditions: One person arrives at checkpoint and has hands in pocket. After repeated commands he takes them out and has a wallet in his hands. Role player takes his hands out in a regular fashion, not slow and not fast.

# of Role Players Needed: 1

Equipment/Props: Native clothing, wallet

Talking Points:

Legal aspects

Is he a threat? Can he be dangerous?

Use of cover

Ramifications if deadly force is used, escalation of force

Scenario 2

Shoot or No-Shoot: Shoot

Set-Up/Conditions: Two Host-Nation Personnel (HN PAX) come to checkpoint. One person is moaning and holding his stomach. They want access to the hospital because the person is injured. Injured person remains disoriented and non responsive. The helper breaks free from injured one and creates distance; injured party takes weapon from inside his clothes and shoots.

# of Role Players Needed: 2

Equipment/Props: Native clothing, weapon

Talking Points:

Legal aspects

Who is a threat?

Use of cover

Ramifications if deadly force is used, escalation of force

Can you shoot "injured" person?

Scenario 3

Shoot or No-Shoot: Shoot

Set-Up/Conditions: Two HN PAX come to checkpoint. One person is moaning and holding his stomach. They want access to the hospital because the person is injured. Injured person remains disoriented and non responsive. The injured one shoots from around the person who is carrying him. The person who is carrying the injured person has no weapon.

# of Role Players Needed: 2

Equipment/Props: Native clothing, weapon

Talking Points:

Legal aspects

Who is a threat? Can you shoot person carrying the other?

Use of cover

Ramifications if deadly force is used, escalation of force

Scenario 4

Shoot or No-Shoot: Shoot

Set-Up/Conditions: Give checkpoint team an interpreter prior to start. Two HN PAX come to checkpoint and speak only Arabic, one has a backpack on. They engage in conversation based upon the team's questions thru the interpreter. The HN PAX have documentation but no valid picture ID (if asked, the interpreter will indicate that something seems not right with the documents). The HN PAX become more disruptive and one pulls out a cell phone and says, "I have a bomb and am going to blow everyone up."

# of Role Players Needed: 2

Equipment/Props: Native clothing, backpack, cell phone

Talking Points:

Legal aspects

Who is a threat?

Use of cover

Scenario 5

Shoot or No-Shoot: Shoot

Set-Up/Conditions: Two HN PAX come to checkpoint at different times. They don't appear to be together. One goes for a weapon.

# of Role Players Needed: 2

Equipment/Props: Native clothing, weapon

Talking Points:

Legal aspects

Who is a threat?

Use of cover

Scenario 6

Shoot or No-Shoot: Shoot

Set-Up/Conditions: Three HN PAX come to checkpoint, kind of together. One is neutral/compliant, one is aggressive/non-compliant, and one is hanging out in back. The one loitering in back leaves the group and then engages the checkpoint team when he creates distance.

# of Role Players Needed: 3

Equipment/Props: Native clothing, weapon

Talking Points:

Legal aspects

Who is a threat?

Use of cover

Suggested Guidelines/Situational Brief before Conducting Exercises:

Pick a TL

Guarding a military checkpoint with access to a FOB

Locals with proper ID can come thru, proper IDs are ones with a picture of that person (mil, LEO, driver's license)

Can call higher if needed

No interpreters at site

No one is allowed to loiter around area, within 50 feet

All persons granting access to FOB will be searched

Normal procedures are to halt prior, establish identity, react accordingly to situation

CHECKPOINT-VEHICULAR

Scenario 1

Shoot or No-Shoot: No shoot

Set-Up/Conditions: Driver is upset and angry about getting hassled at gate and makes furtive movement to get his ID in the glove box. Occupants are not in native clothing or in military uniform.

# of Role Players Needed: Minimum 2 (one driver, one passenger)

Equipment/Props: Vehicle, ID

Talking Points:

Legal aspects

Verbal commands

Positioning by vehicle

Who is a threat?

Use of cover

Reading of body language, movements, eye contact of people

Scenario 2

Shoot or No-Shoot: No shoot

Set-Up/Conditions: Contractors arrive at checkpoint and give proper ID to gain entry. Weapons are visible in vehicle.

# of Role Players Needed: 2 to 3

Equipment/Props: Vehicle, weapons, ID for each

Talking Points:

Legal aspects

Verbal commands

Positioning by vehicle

Who is a threat?

Use of cover

Reading of body language, movements, eye contact of people

Scenario 3

Shoot or No-Shoot: Shoot

Set-Up/Conditions: Vehicle being detained for identification and another party (that is dismounted), not related to occupants, start firing (from a concealed position) at the checkpoint control team.

    # of Role Players Needed: 4 to 5 (2 to 3 in vehicle and 2 dismounted)

    Equipment/Props: Vehicle, weapons, ID for each in vehicle

    Talking Points:

Legal aspects

Verbal commands

Positioning by vehicle

Who is a threat?

Use of cover

Reading of body language, movements, eye contact of people

Scenario 4

Shoot or No-Shoot: ?

Set-Up/Conditions: A vehicle arrives at a checkpoint to gain entry. A person/civilian/bystander walks to an adjacent area and leaves a bag and then walks away.

    # of Role Players Needed: 3 (2 in vehicle, 1 dismounted)

    Equipment/Props: Vehicle, proper ID for each, backpack

    Talking Points:

Legal aspects

Verbal commands

Positioning by vehicle

Who is a threat?

Use of cover

Reading of body language, movements, eye contact of people
Actions with bag?

Scenario 5
Shoot or No-Shoot: Shoot
Set-Up/Conditions: Vehicle arrives at checkpoint for entry. A passenger, who is hidden, jumps out of the vehicle and starts shooting.
# of Role Players Needed: 3
Equipment/Props: Vehicle, weapon
Talking Points:
Legal aspects
Verbal commands
Positioning by vehicle
Who is a threat?
Use of cover
Reading of body language, movements, eye contact of people

Suggested Guidelines/Situational Brief before Conducting Exercises:
Pick a TL
Guarding a military checkpoint with access to a FOB
Locals with proper ID can come thru, proper IDs are ones with a picture of that person (mil, LEO, driver's license)
Can call higher if needed
No interpreters at site
No one is allowed to loiter around area, within 50 feet
All vehicles that are not contractors or military will be searched
All vehicles CAN be searched dependent upon discretion of TL
Normal procedures are to halt prior, establish identity, react accordingly to situation

SPECIAL
Scenario 1: Special-office/financial
Shoot or No-Shoot: No shoot
Set-Up/Conditions: The office is set up to reimburse claims that have been caused by coalition forces. There is a line of 3 HN PAX waiting for

the Army rep to pay them. 1st PAX is paid without incident. 2nd PAX is not satisfied and starts yelling.

# of Role Players Needed: 3

Equipment/Props: Native clothing for each, papers for each, ID for each, office set up with desk and chairs, money, control log

Talking Points:

Legal aspects

Who is a threat?

Reading of body language, movements, eye contact of people

Remarks:

Don't feel cheated if you do not fire

Course is centered on identification of threats not on tactics

Contact shots are okay but do not fire, instructors will assess

We shoot until when??? (Shoot them into the ground!)

Use whatever force is necessary that you feel is justified

Use good contact-cover principles, obtain situational awareness, take control of the situation, act like they are real events, make it real

Variables:

Innocent bystander in the way

Contractors entering with proper identification

More people within scenarios

Engagement distances

Talking points:

Internal SOPs, living documents

Threat assessment

Situational awareness-knowing when you are vulnerable, understanding the strengths and weaknesses of you and your enemy

Situations are fluid, one slight deviation in the scenario may result in an entirely different response

Nothing is 100% risk free

You can do everything correct and have bad things happen, you can do everything wrong and have a positive outcome

By knowing your strengths and weaknesses (situational awareness) you
are better prepared to make good decisions and mitigate risk

REFERENCES
Patrick, Urey and Hall, John C., *In Defense of Self and Others*, 2005.
Grossman, Dave, *On Combat*, 2004.
Murray, Kenneth, Getting Firearms Training out of the Range using
Specialized Munitions.
Simunition International Training Division, Advanced Instructor
Course, February 1998
Smith & Wesson Academy, Contemporary Issues of Use of Force
Management 1993 Cooper, Jeff, American Pistol Institute, 1995